God's Waiting Room

God's Waiting Room

The Pathway from Despair to Hope

LISÂNIAS MOURA

Translated by
Laurie Carpenter

CIP-Brasil. Catalogação na publicação
Sindicato Nacional dos Editores de Livros, RJ

M887g

Moura, Lisânias

God's waiting room : the pathway from despair to hope
/ Lisânias Moura ; tradução Laurie Anne Carpenter. - 1. ed. -
São Paulo : Mundo Cristão, 2024.
128 p.

Tradução de: A sala de espera de Deus
ISBN 978-65-5988-345-5

1. Esperança - Aspectos religiosos - Cristianismo. 2.
Sofrimento - Meditação. 3. Fé. I. Carpenter, Laurie Anne.
II. Título.

24-92520   CDD: 234.2
                                            CDU: 27-423.79

Gabriela Faray Ferreira Lopes - Bibliotecária - CRB-7/6643

Editorial production
MC Team

Cover
Jonatas Belan

Published in Brazil with all
rights reserved by:
Editora Mundo Cristão
Rua Antônio Carlos Tacconi, 69
São Paulo, SP, Brazil
ZIP 04810-020
Phone: 55 11 2127-4147
www.mundocristao.com.br

Category: Christian Life
1st edition: August 2019

To Teca, my faithful companion in the waiting rooms of life.
To God, for giving me Teca as wife.

Contents

Acknowledgments

To my beloved community, the Morumbi Baptist Church. In these 26 years together, your affection for my family and me have been a source of encouragement during our moments in waiting rooms.

To my two sons, Daniel and Rafael, a unique part of our waiting rooms, in a loving, patient and meaningful way.

To each family in our church, who has shared with us their dilemmas, pains and joys. They encourage us and help us to learn to trust God in the long times of silence and waiting.

To Maurício Zágari, editor of Editora Mundo Cristão. Thank you for being present, encouraging me, giving feedback, improving the texts from beginning to end of each project and helping me grow and write better.

Introdução

In the way of the waiting room

A waiting room can become one of the loneliest places in the world, even if you are surrounded by many people. It could be a waiting room in a hospital, a company where you have gone for a job interview, or even in a restaurant. Regardless of the place, waiting in such a place makes us uncomfortable because biding one's time isn't pleasant. Regardless of whether the time spent there is short or long, sad or happy, apprehensive or peaceful, when we are forced to wait for something we often lack virtues such as patience, peace, wisdom, and trust.

How can we survive in a waiting room?

Pedro and Dora 's son was admitted to a hospital after suffering a severe seizure. João Carlos had created an app with two of his colleagues, but was betrayed by a supposedly Christian investor, who took over his idea. Joás and Celina waited more than five years to get married, they remained sexually pure for each other, but after three years of marriage, Joás left her to live in a same-sex relationship. Joubert suffered a car accident while driving to a theological seminary, where he would study to dedicate himself to preaching the gospel in the mission field.

Pedro, Dora, João Carlos, Joás, Celina, and Joubert all had something in common. They were all encouraged to pray and heard platitudes like: "God has a wonderful plan for your life," "Don't be discouraged, just pray and trust, for God is sovereign" and "God writes straight using crooked lines." How can we possibly understand that the Lord often leaves us waiting in a cold, lonely room where time seems to have stopped? Is God really sovereign and in control? Is God actually good?

The stories I tell in this book are actual cases that I heard in my pastoral office, although the names have been changed. I have also personally been in God's waiting room and experienced the shudders that it often provokes. In the fifth month of pregnancy with our second child, the gynecologist advised me and my wife, Teca, that our baby would probably die during childbirth. And it got even worse when the doctor said that "both mother and son could die during delivery." That began was five months in a dark waiting room, facing something we weren't prepared for.

> How do you survive in the waiting room when the outlook isn't good? How can we expect God to answer our prayers when it seems like they are falling on deaf ears?

How do you survive in the waiting room when the outlook isn't good? How can we expect God to answer our prayers when it seems like they are falling on deaf ears? How do we stay positive in the waiting room when all we hear is: "Pray and everything will work out," but the "everything" doesn't seem to be working out? Where is God in all of this?

While we are in the waiting room, it seems like the clock has stopped, the door doesn't open and the people around us do not understand our pain. Often, people try to encourage us, but their words only reveal platitudes that do not generate faith, such as "Everything will be fine," "God is in control" or

"God knows all things." We already know that often things will work out, that the Lord is in control of everything and that he is omniscient. But in what manner and how long do we need to stay in the waiting room before the waiting makes sense?

The prophet Habakkuk had a life-changing experience in a waiting room. Under the rule of King Josiah, he saw the kingdom of Judah prosper, a small revival take place, and eventually the nation collapse. Josiah brought about spiritual, social, and political reforms, sparked a temporary revival in the nation, and became known as a great reformer. But when Jehoahaz, Josiah's son, took the throne, he disregarded the ways of the Lord, following the paths of sin of his forefathers. This grieved Habakkuk's soul.

The book of Habakkuk expresses the prophet's anguish. His nation should have acted as a sign of God's presence in the world, but the prophet was distressed to see people moving further and further away from the Lord. Religion cloaked in immorality and corruption became the culture of its people. Over time, it was obvious that the population of Judah had grown spiritually cold; it exchanged the God of the covenant for the false gods of the neighboring peoples.

There was violence, impunity of its leaders, a weakening of the justice system, and the wicked triumphed over those who wanted to please God. Although Habakkuk should have prophesied to Judah in the name of God, the pain of the nation's situation caused the prophet to reverse the communication. He began to interrogate God and no longer acted as a spokesman for the Lord to his people.

In this process of talking to God about himself and about what he saw, the prophet longed for answers and for improvements in the life of the covenant nation. But, contrary to his expectations, he only witnessed the collapse of Judah. In an attempt to resolve the situation, Habakkuk questioned God from the depths of his soul, but God did not seem to hear him.

Nevertheless, the fact that Habakkuk spoke more about the people to God than of God to the people did not diminish the importance of the prophet's message. Neither does it bring into question the inspiration of his book. The truth is that it translates for people today some of the deepest yearnings of human beings, including that of understanding God when divine ways do not make sense to the human mind. That is why the book of Habakkuk is so crucial for our us today. Written over 25 centuries ago, it contains the revelation of God that sustains us and moves us from despair to hope.

Individuals, families, and churches often find themselves amid unexpected chaos. It could be the chaos of a divorce, an incurable illness, an abruptly destroyed career, a financial failure, or a division in the congregation. Praying is the first suggestion of action. But often it seems like our prayers don't reach God and waiting on Him becomes a perplexing experience. Sometimes divine answers don't seem to make any sense. It often feels like God has placed us in a lonely, painful, dark waiting room, the walls of which are adorned with unanswered questions.

"The truth is that sitting in the waiting room can create a hardened heart or one full of faith. In it we find a God that we would never discover in a brightly lit party room full of happy people. By applying the writings of the prophet Habakkuk to today's culture, we discover that God relates personally to his children and leads them from despair to hope, even when the waiting room seems unnerving or just too time consuming." Overcome by agony and fear, the prophet retires to a tower, a waiting room, and challenges us to do the same, believing that

God is with us, even if the wait is long. We see that not only is it possible to find God amid the despair, but that he never abandons us in those moments. Although he may appear to be silent, he is always active, for the God of Israel does not sleep. Despite loneliness and fear, Habakkuk lived there without despair, austerely dealing with his questions even though there weren't apparent answers.

You and I have something in common with Habakkuk, Pedro, Dora, João Carlos, Joás, Celina and Joubert. We all ask questions when we are struggling and facing paths that seem stony and difficult. How can we survive in a world that is going from bad to worse, where evil seems to overcome good, and where the corrupt and the unjust laugh at God and yet the Lord appears to be silent?

In the months between the conversation with the gynecologist and the day our son was born, my wife and I often stared at the clock in the waiting room, fearing the passage of time. After all, every hour that passed brought us closer to the moment when we would know whether the doctor's prediction would come true. We wavered between confidence and anxiety. What if our baby died? And I avoided asking the question that tormented my soul: "And what if my wife dies?" We were constantly confronted by the question: "What do we really want? Relief or the glory of God?"

> We see that not only is it possible to find God amid the despair, but that he never abandons us in those moments.

There was a time in human history when people believed that things would get better. The progress of science and international relations seemed to improve. The great technological discoveries proposed a healthier, safer, and more productive lifestyle. The proposed use of computers and smartphones apparently promised a life with less stress and fewer working hours, aiming to benefit human beings by multiplying time for family life and leisure. But reality turned out to be very different from the imagined scenario. The real world brought broken families, increased loneliness, individualism and violence, and the dissemination of hopelessness, anxiety, and despair. Humanity continues to fluctuate between hope and horror. We yearn for answers and paths that can lead us from anxiety to peace, from fear to security, from despair to hope.

Is it possible for Pedro, Dora, João Carlos, Joás, Celina, Joubert, and you and me to live in a healthy way in a world marked by so many evils? Is it possible to see things get worse in the world and, sometimes, in our lives and still not lose focus on God? Can we continue to believe that he is good and not resort to empty triumphalist theology that runs away from pain and failures because we don't want to suffer?

In this book, I wish to show that Habakkuk's message demonstrates there is hope in life's waiting rooms. By turning to God amid despair, the prophet was able to conclude: "The Sovereign Lord is my strength! He makes me as surefooted as a deer, able to tread upon the heights" (Hab. 3:19). But how did he live between the moment when he uttered, "How long, O Lord, must I call for help? But you do not listen!" (1:2) and the moment when he affirmed "yet I will rejoice in the Lord! I will be joyful in the God of my salvation!" (3:18)?

Habakkuk discovered that in the waiting rooms of life, where fear and anxiety dwell, God, and God alone, could lead him from despair to hope. And though we may experience despair, we shouldn't be consumed by it. For the same God that Habakkuk heard listens to you and me.

I invite you to learn from Habakkuk about how God comes to us in times of loneliness and is powerful enough to change our history. My hope is that you find yourself with the same God that the prophet encountered, for the Lord has the power to transform chaos into grace and love.

On this journey, don't forget that while you languish in the waiting room, God has not left you alone. Even if the silence is long, even if the Lord seems to have abandoned you, he is leading you from despair to hope.

1

In the Waiting Room with a Silent God

Does God really answer our prayers?

Most babies are still asleep at half past five in the morning. Dora was just getting up to give Teodoro his first feeding of the day, when she heard a strange choking sound coming from her son's room. She ran to see what was going on and found her baby writhing in convulsions. Dora screamed for her husband Pedro, who jumped out of bed and grabbed the baby out of the crib. Not knowing what to do, he simply cried out: "God, have mercy on us!"

The convulsions only lasted for about twenty seconds after Pedro had pulled Teodoro out of his crib, but for Pedro and Dora, it was as if they had dragged on for hours. The baby seemed to be unconscious and the couple rushed him to the hospital. As first-time parents, they were stunned, unsure, and desperate. The ride from their house to the hospital was only about fifteen minutes, but it felt like fifteen hours.

They anxiously entered the emergency room, and practically screamed for help. A nurse took the baby in her arms and said in an assertive tone, "Go to the waiting room. I'll talk to you again shortly." The room was empty, and the chairs were disarranged as if it had been used by a crowd hours before. The glass on the wall clock was cracked. Nearby there was a door bearing a sign: "No Unauthorized Access." Pedro and

Dora knew that someone would come through that door to give them news about Teodoro.

As they waited, questions ran through their minds. "What had happened?" "Why?" and "How long will it take to receive news on our son?" Dora thought back over Teodoro's life. She'd had trouble conceiving, and after four years of trying, she'd finally gotten pregnant. Her gynecologist had told her it would be a miracle if she conceived, so she was certain it was a miracle from God. During the pregnancy, the baby had almost died, but the whole church had prayed with them and he had survived.

They waited anxiously for the door to open. The silence and solitude of the waiting room seemed to contribute to the couple's state of anxiety and despair. The two prayed, but God seemed to remain distant and silent. They cried out, but it seemed no one heard them. Where was God now? And why didn't that restricted access hospital door open with good news about Teodoro? The door seemed like the entrance to a fortress: cold, heavy, and immovable. Dora asked Pedro, "How long will we have to wait?"

Habakkuk also dealt with a desperate situation that he never imagined having to face. The prophet knew that he served the only God and that he was part of the chosen people. This most likely made him feel protected, for he believed that nothing bad could happen to God's beloved people. But the situation surprised him. In his rant, Habakkuk showed his dissatisfaction, anxiety, and despair brought on by the state of the nation and God's apparent distance.

Don't we sometimes find ourselves in similar situations? Even though we are saved by God's grace and we've walked with Christ for years, knowing his character, power, and grace, we can find ourselves in unimaginable situations. We are hit by a catastrophe and suddenly feel totally helpless and over-whelmed with doubts.

Habakkuk revealed his anguish to God. Often, our despair comes as a result of our inability to understand God's actions. For a Jew, receiving divine punishment through an idola-trous, violent, and immoral people was deeply humiliating. Even more so because, as a prophet, Habakkuk knew Deu-teronomy 28:15-68. In these verses God makes it clear that obedience brings blessings, and disobedience results in dis-cipline. He knew that the Lord keeps his promises, not only the promises of blessings, but also the disciplinary ones and so he experienced a sense of despair and helplessness, aggra-vated by Judah's spiritual coldness and the immoral lives of the nation's leaders.

The Babylonian invasion would certainly bring chaos to Ju-dah in several areas. The nation's economy would be deeply affected, its leadership would be humiliated, and the people would be taken into slavery. What could Habakkuk do in this situation? He was a prophet; yet, just like us, he was subject to all the fears and insecurities in situations over which we have no control or which we do not understand.

Habakkuk's emotions surfaced and were reflected in his attitude as he addressed the Lord. His first emotional expres-sion is marked by his impression that he was talking to a silent God, who neither listens nor acts in favor of his serv-ent. Pedro and Dora experienced the same sensation in that waiting room. They prayed, deliberated, cried out, watched the clock and still… nothing. It didn't seem as though ito was the same God that they had known all these years, through faith in Jesus.

When God is silent

Habakkuk asks God: "How long, O LORD, must I call for help? But you do not listen! 'Violence is everywhere!' I cry, but you do not come to save" (1:2). In other words, it was as if the prophet were asking, "Lord, why are you silent?"

It's so hard when we run to the Lord in the midst of adversity or when we are under pressure, but feel disconnected from Him. We get the sensation that we are facing a God who is mute, deaf, and distant.

It wasn't just Habakkuk who experienced the frigidity of a waiting room. Heman, the author of Psalm 88, also experienced similar moments. "O LORD, God of my salvation, I cry out to you by day. I come to you at night. Now hear my prayer; listen to my cry. For my life is

> Often, our despair is the result of an inability to understand God's actions.

full of troubles, and death draws near" (Psalm 88:1-3). Heman voices his lament in a desperate tone. Notice how similar his inner situation is to Habakkuk's: "O LORD, I cry out to you. I will keep on pleading day by day. O LORD, why do you reject me? Why do you turn your face from me?" (Psalm 88:13-14).

Like the prophet of Judah, the psalmist faced a time of pain and a feeling of abandonment, including on the part of God. But like Habakkuk, he decides not to let his feelings paralyze him. Rather, he decides to act and run to God. In the depths of their anguish, both prophet and psalmist cry out to the Lord and pour out their hearts.

When the prophet says: "How long...,"[1] it is assumed that for quite some time he has been asking God to help him understand the situation or even to intervene, yet the Almighty has not responded to his cries. In the biblical text, the verb "to cry"[2] reveals an expectation that the Lord will act and intervene. But from the prophet's perspective, God was cold and distant. The issue was not so much God's silence as the fact that he seemed unresponsive. According to the prophet, things were stagnant: "The law has become paralyzed, and there is no justice in the courts" (Habakkuk 1:4).[3]

The prophet's anxiety was due to the law being ignored and God's apparent indifference to the situation. Many who kneel beside the bed of a sick loved one waiting for a cure that takes a long time or perhaps never occurs have experienced the Lord's delay and their unanswered prayers. It is the same plight experienced by an unemployed follower of Jesus who is accumulating overdue bills while continually praying for a job offer. It is also the experience of a father who pleads for the sanity of his child who is increasingly addicted to drugs, but who fails to see God intervening.

The fact is that all of us, whether we like it or not, sooner or later will experience days when God seems silent. We will be discouraged by endless delays, which can lead to anxiety and even despair. So how do we deal with these times?

Mercy, grace, and love are all part of God's character, as is his faithfulness. And precisely because we know him, we can never interpret his silence as inactivity, but instead we should rest and wait. In times of apparent silence, God intervenes in our journey and observes us attentively. The fact is that it is possible to perceive God's silence incorrectly, since we may not clearly understand his actions.

One truth we need to keep in mind in the days, months, or years of God's silence is that during that time, the Lord is transforming our lives. The time in life's waiting rooms is a period of inner transformation. The Father, who loves us with an incomprehensible love, wishes to transform us; transformation is necessary and takes time. God works in silence, because it is in silence that we learn that the Lord transforms despair into hope. Even God's closest friends are not exempt from experiencing his silence. Habakkuk experienced this silence even after crying out to God for a long time. But, without his realizing it, the Lord was molding a new heart in him.

Pedro and Dora stared at the waiting room door, expecting it to open at any moment. But nothing happened, no news arrived. They might not have realized it, but God was turning their anxiety and despair into an experience of grace. The couple could not see what was going on behind that closed door and, seized by anxiety and fear, continued asking, "How much longer, Lord?" But God was there, acting on behalf of little Teodoro.

Habakkuk wasn't the only one who discovered God in the midst of silence. Abraham also spent many years in God's waiting room, waiting for his promises to be fulfilled. And so did Joseph, son of Jacob. It is estimated that more than 15 years passed between the day of Joseph's dream that revealed the Lord's plans for his life and the moment when he took over the second most important position in Egypt. The fact is that God is not forgetful nor inactive. Could he have fulfilled his purposes in the lives of Abraham and Joseph in less time? Of course. He is almighty! But *God acts on behalf of all those he loves even when he is silent.*

At that moment in Habakkuk's life, however, God's silence in response to his cries didn't seem to make any sense. The prophet's human perception was of God's total absence. But our misconception of God's processes does not cause him to change his plans nor turn his clock forward when there is no reason to. The Lord is constantly active, working for his own glory and for the accomplishment of his purposes in his time. And certainly, when his will is fulfilled, we are the beneficiaries.

When Habakkuk expresses his feelings to God, two issues become clear. First, the prophet has a unique freedom with the Lord to say what he feels. We must understand that God does not forbid us to feel anything. We can't help feeling desolate and hopeless or even that God is distant from us. But we can overcome this feeling by preventing it from falsely becoming the reality that controls us.

Habakkuk was free to experience these bad feelings, but he did not allow himself to be dominated by them. The prophet shared his feelings with God, and this is a tremendous lesson for us. The Lord does not despise our emotions, nor is he intimidated or hurt when we express our feelings. God knew that Habakkuk would react this way when he faced the nation's circumstances and that he would question him about it. Yet the prophet's real, emotional, and logical questions did not make him change his plans. The same is true for us.

God did not stop Habakkuk from treading that path. Even though the prophet did not know the direction of his journey, the Lord knew where he wanted to lead him. This was as difficult for Habakkuk as it was for Joseph, for Pedro and Dora, and for me and my wife. Why does God allow us to go through uncertain moments when he himself knows the suffering we will face? Isn't he our Father? Could it be that, as our Father, he does not have all the power to prevent us from suffering?

It is precisely because God is our Father that he allows us to go through seemingly bewildering moments. After all, when we surrender ourselves to the Lord in these difficult periods, the waiting room becomes an instrument for perfecting our faith. God always wants the best for his children, which is why, as our Father, he sometimes gives us apparently incoherent gifts, even at the risk of not being understood.

We can question God and express our emotions inappropriately, but none of this phases the Lord nor makes him give up on leading us where he wants. Today, we may feel desolate or desperate, but the destination to which God wants to lead us—even when he seems silent or absent—is much more significant and exceptional than what we see or contemplate.

Teodoro's parents couldn't walk through the waiting room door, no matter how much they wanted to. The doctors weren't Teodoro's parents, but Pedro and Dora didn't have the necessary expertise to treat their son's illness. As his parents, they wanted to save him, but it would have been presumptuous for them to think they knew more than the doctors. We often want to do the same with God. Our anxiety suggests that we know how to resolve things better than he does; thus, we think that the Lord is taking too long to act or resolve the problem. Often, though, it is in silence and delay that God prepares something wonderful for our lives or through our lives.

Habakkuk poured out all his feelings to God. He lamented the Lord's delay and naturally expected an answer. But was God's answer what the prophet expected?

Does God always answer the way we expect him to?

Habakkuk's prayer created an expectation that God would answer. When we pray, we also expect the Lord to answer us by delivering us from our agonies. Based on his knowledge of God and of his past actions, Habakkuk was convinced that God would quickly respond to his heartfelt and sincere prayer. Furthermore, when we pray about a problem or because we are desperate, we expect the Lord to intervene supernaturally, especially if we feel helpless. Our impatience prevents us from seeing God's long term plans.

Habakkuk's actions are no different than ours when we face soul struggles and present them to the Lord. The phrase "God is faithful" sounds like a mantra when we are desperate and expect the divine action that we imagine or would like. Saying "God is in control" is another supposedly spiritual way of running away from problems and questions we don't have answers to. These statements are true, but they are not mantras that will automatically rid us of our fear or make us immediately feel safe and peaceful.

I imagine that in his time of spiritual drought, the phrase Job most looked forward to hearing God say was, "Job, I'm going to heal you." Joseph may have wished for God's quick intervention in his situation. Both Job and Joseph may have thought that since they were faithful to God, his answer would bring them quick relief. But they both still had very valuable lessons to learn in God's waiting room. They still had a long road ahead of them before they would become what the Lord wanted for them.

While they waited for the door to open, Pedro and Dora had no idea what God wanted to produce in their lives. Their greatest desire was the relief of hearing the doctors tell them that their son was fine. Likewise, Habakkuk longed for the Lord's healing intervention for his people and, consequently, for himself. But what if God's answer isn't what we expect?

Sometimes God's answers to our prayers are what we expect; other times not. Sometimes God's answers are understandable; other times they seem to suggest that he doesn't understand our language. Yet in no way does this mean that God is deaf or that he ignores what we say. The Lord just wants to prepare us for something beyond our understanding, in his own time.

This what happens when God breaks his silence and tells Habakkuk to watch what is happening. Although Habakkuk did not realize it, the answer had been in preparation for some time. Regardless of the chaos, we will always encounter encouraging touches of grace that keep us from stumbling. Pedro and Dora had many questions and concerns, but they didn't fully realize that behind that door was a medical team working on Teodoro's behalf. When the disciples were afraid during the notorious storm on the Sea of Galilee, they didn't realize that the simple fact that Jesus was in the boat with them was the ultimate sign that God would answer their prayers. In the midst of chaotic storms, we must never forget that God remains with us.

Between the end of the prophet Malachi's ministry and the birth of Jesus, God seemed to remain silent, when in reality he was preparing the world for the arrival of the Messiah. In those approximately 400 years of silence, the world acquired a world-wide language (Greek) and this opened channels of communication so that the good news of Jesus Christ could be understood not only by those who spoke Hebrew, but by most of the world in the Asia Minor region at the time. Furthermore, it was in this period of silence that God elevated a new world power, Rome, responsible for building roads that would be traveled by persecuted Christians for spreading the gospel throughout the world. It was also through the Roman Empire that God installed the so-called *pax romana*, a political and military environment that favored the propagation of the message of the cross. In silence, God works and creates the necessary circumstances to communicate the wonders of his grace to us and to the world.

Here is God's answer to the prophet: "Look around at the nations; look and be amazed!" (Habakkuk 1:5). In other words, it was as if he were saying, "Look, I am already taking action!" In God's own words, his action was worthy of admiration. In fact, God uses a command. The people of Jerusalem were to be amazed, astonished, and perplexed by the impact of the news.

> In silence, God works and creates the necessary circumstances to communicate the wonders of his grace to us and to the world.

God also had a message for the lost, corrupt, and immoral people. The Lord made clear his opposition to this situation, but the people were blinded by their sin and were unable to see God's actions.

In this same message, God addresses Habakkuk. His words are unexpected, surprising, enigmatic, and shocking: "I am raising up the Babylonians, a cruel and violent people. They will march across the world and conquer other lands" (Habakkuk 1:6).[4] The prophet responds: "O LORD my God, my Holy One, you who are eternal—surely you do not plan to wipe us out? O LORD, our Rock, you have sent these Babylonians to correct us, to punish us for our many sins" (Habakkuk 1:12).

So here we have Habakkuk praying, lamenting his emotional state and that of the nation, asking God to break his silence, and the Lord's response is overwhelmingly negative. It was as if Habakkuk and the people had asked for bread and God gave them a stone. It was as if they had cried out for deliverance and transformation and God answered, "It will get worse." Initially this was the meaning of God's answer. But it also pointed to something that would ultimately be wonderful for all mankind.

Have you ever been in a similar situation? Have you ever tirelessly interceded to God on behalf of a sick family member you loved, but they ended up dying anyway? The door to Peter and Dora's waiting room finally opened. The nurse emerged with empty hands. She said, "The baby's condition is delicate. Wait a little longer and the doctor will come talk to you."

I remember well the hours I spent waiting while my wife was in the delivery room. They were hours of anxiety, in dead silence. Just me and God. I was afraid and I had many questions. Especially, "What if God doesn't answer my prayers?"

Habakkuk's expression "You who are eternal surely don't plan to exterminate us," can be read as either a statement or a question. Viewed as a question, it is rhetorical and does not necessarily need an answer. But what if Habakkuk was actually asking God, "How is it that the Lord, being eternal, decides to use the immoral, violent, corrupt, and spiteful Babylonians against us?" Wasn't it too insolent for Habakkuk to talk to God like this? Wouldn't it be spiritually immature to question God like this?

Habakkuk's concept of eternity implies seeing God as the one who knows everything, has power over everything, and can do whatever he wishes. But, even though he is the Lord, it would be asking too much of the prophet to accept a divine plan that involved using the Babylonians as an instrument to punish God's chosen people. But even after hearing the forceful and detailed description of the Babylonians' violent, idolatrous, and destructive character, the prophet understood that God did not intend to exterminate his people.

It is interesting to note that Habakkuk was at the same time both bold and respectful toward God. Would we have the courage to talk to the Lord like that? There was a tone of disappointment with God, but also of trust. Habakkuk could speak, and the Lord did not despise the prophet or his words.

One of the hardest things to admit in the Christian life is that we can become disappointed with God. Saying that "God is faithful" in the midst of despair, without acknowledging the pain, means to hide our anger and disappointment. But Habakkuk knew the faithful and loving God, and so he felt comfortable expressing the depths of his emotions to him, without worrying about whether his theology was correct. The prophet knew that he could pour himself out before the Lord without fear of being rejected.

A theology that doesn't allow us to be ourselves and stand freely before God is not healthy. Habakkuk's theology was pure, sincere, respectful, and courageous, simply because he knew that he was accepted and loved by the Lord regardless of whether he understood and questioned God's plans. The prophet's understanding was the fruit of his having experienced grace in his life. And it was the beginning of the journey from despair to hope.

In God's love we find the freedom to question Him. The violence in Jerusalem made Habakkuk question God, especially because a holy God is not compatible with immorality and corruption. But the Lord is sovereign to act as he wills.

The author of Hebrews exhorts us to appear before God with *confidence*:[5] "And so, dear brothers and sisters, we can boldly enter heaven's Most Holy Place because of the blood of Jesus" (Hebrews 10:19). The word *confidence* (*parrhesia* in Greek) can be translated as "boldness," "courage," "freedom," "free expression of speech," "fearlessness." We can be transparent before the Lord and question Him about what is distressing us. Like Habakkuk, we can have the courage to ask and to disagree. We can cry before God and fearlessly say, "I have lost my faith in you." Nothing prevents us from coming to the Lord fully as we are, without protocol or rituals. Simply, because of our faith in Jesus, we can appear before God and express our perplexity when we do not understand his actions in our lives.

One of the components of the faith that impacts us most is God's merciful grace when our emotions are out of control. Instead of feeling rejected, our fear is transformed into hope because of God's unconditional love. We can enter the presence of the Lord and weep copiously, with the confidence that we will be embraced.

Habakkuk was bold and transparent. In a very vulnerable way, he acknowledged God's holiness in using the Babylonians, even though it was hard for him to understand. When we are in the holy of holies—in the intimate presence of God—and we pour out our fears, worries, disappointments, or anger, Paul's words come alive: "Don't worry about anything; instead, pray about everything. Tell God what you need, and thank him for all he has done. Then you will experience God's peace, which exceeds anything we can understand. His peace will guard your hearts and minds as you live in Christ Jesus" (Philippians 4:6-7).

IN THE WAITING ROOM WITH A SILENT GOD

Holy and eternal is our Rock

Habakkuk questioned God, but at no time did he consider turning away from Him. This is evident when he calls God "my Holy One" (1:12). Even though he was faced with the violence, corruption, and immorality of his people and found out that the Lord was going to use an even worse people to punish them, Habakkuk did not lose sight of who God is and the characteristics of his character.

Habakkuk approaches God with the knowledge of his character. Because he is holy, God would not let his people be exterminated, nor would he fail in his promises to Abraham. After all, a holy God cannot lie. Habakkuk's expression, "my Holy One" is very significant. His misconception of God's processes did not prevent the prophet from continuing to look to the Lord with intimacy and trust, nor did it generate in Habakkuk an uncontrollable despair, to the point of losing confidence in the Father of the nation. This is quite evident because, before referring to God as "my Holy One," Habakkuk calls him "Lord," *Yahweh*, the God of the covenant with the nation and with Abraham. *Yahweh* is the Lord of everything in the universe and nothing escapes his control. God is *Yahweh*, but he is also a personal God, "my Holy One." He does not cease to be holy because he uses a reprehensible nation to accomplish his purposes. *Yahweh* is the beginning of all things, the all-sufficient, all-powerful God who knows the plight of the people and the heart of the prophet.

When we find ourselves in a desperate situation or feel helpless to deal with certain circumstances, what we need most is this God who is Lord of the universe and who remains our personal God. *Welcoming us into his presence, even when we are angry, is grace.* And this grace comes through Jesus.

"My Holy One" doesn't need me to understand him. We are not called to understand God, but to trust and obey him, even in incomprehensible situations. He will always be holy. What I need is to be understood by *Yahweh.* And he understands me. In fact, I need to believe that by his grace *Yahweh* accepts me and puts up with my follies. It is this understanding that provides ultimate assurance to the prophet. The situation he and his people face would potentially be disastrous, but it was not final.

> Welcoming us into his presence, even when we are angry, is grace.

At this point in Habakkuk's dialogue with God, we notice another one of the prophet's attributes that teaches us and serves as a beacon for the days of rough seas or complete fog in the waiting room. Instead of thinking "there is no point in continuing to focus on God" or even contemplating the idea of rethinking his way of imagining the Lord, Habakkuk recognizes his helplessness in the face of chaos. By calling God "my Holy One," the prophet was saying: "You are holy and I am a sinner, so it is better to trust you than to focus on my questions or doubts." If we prefer to discover the cause of despair rather than to put the focus on our holy God—even when we disagree with him or think his ways don't make sense—we will remain in our hopeless state.

The God that Habakkuk saw was also greater than time: "You who are eternal" (1:12). By emphasizing this, the prophet reaffirms his confidence in the Lord: because he is eternal, he does not go away, he does not cease to exist, and he has the necessary time to fulfill his promises. After all, for God, all time is always today.

In moments of despair, we may assume that God is unjust and slow to answer. But the reality is that the Lord's eternal character makes him trustworthy, for he has at his disposal the time needed to show his faithfulness. God's delay in intervening to change the evil doings can grieve us, but precisely because he is eternal and holy, the Lord helps us in his time and in whatever way he sees fit. When we adjust our time to his, God works on our anxiety and breaks our tendency to want to control what we cannot control.

Habakkuk was discovering more about holiness and God's way of working in his own time. The prophet might have been distressed and desperate, but he was on the right track, for when he saw trouble, he ran to God. He could have resisted the Lord's plans and fled, as Jonah did (Jonah 1—4), but he didn't. Not even violence, corruption, and a troublesome response to his prayer made the prophet change his theological and practical worldview. He might not have understood God's process in his life, but he knew it was possible to run to him because of the faithful, holy, and eternal character of the Most High. That is why he calls God "our Rock" (Habakkuk 1:12).[6]

In situations of pressure and despair in waiting rooms, we need a safe harbor, a Rock. The Babylonians were a threat to the prophet and his people; they represented war, loss, suffering, and destruction. Even though Habakkuk questioned God about all of this, he was certain that God was his safe harbor. Knowing the Law, it seems that Habakkuk remembered the words of Moses: "He is the Rock; his deeds are perfect. Everything he does is just and fair. He is a faithful God who does no wrong; how just and upright he is!" (Deuteronomy 32:4).

By calling God "our Rock," the prophet recognizes that God is just and true, even when he judges the nation of Israel by using Babylon. And these divine characteristics create stability in times of insecurity and confusion.

At this point in his dialogue with God, Habakkuk seems to accept and understand that the enemies' actions are the fruit of God's discipline. They are not merely a punitive discipline, but a redemptive one.

Touches of grace are released in moments of solitude in waiting rooms.s. We gain much more by paying attention to them than by impatiently staring at the clock, which only records a misconceived delay in the Lord's answers to our prayers. Surely, one of the greatest touches of God's grace is to lead us to discover more about him, his character, and his redeeming love for us.

By calling God "my holy one" and "our Rock," Habakkuk records the Lord's profound revelation to him. It was as if, by inspiring his prophet to write at that moment, God was telling him, "There is a question you have not asked!" The questions we ask in times of distress reveal much of what is in our heart. If we ask "How long, Lord?" or "Why is the Lord letting me go through all this?," it is clear that our heart is centered on ourselves and not on God's character. Thus, in order to abandon the desire to be the center of attention and to put the focus on God, we need to ask the crucial question, "What does the Lord want to reveal to me about Himself?" This kind of question will never come up when we are relaxing at the edge of a swimming pool, for it is at the point of protracted pain and questioning

> Touches of grace are released in moments of solitude in waiting rooms.

that God calls us to listen to Him. He wants us to discover that in the midst of despair, what we need most is not necessarily to receive relief from fear or a solution to the problem, but rather to discover the holy God who is our Rock. After all, it is his presence that gives us the stability to survive in the waiting rooms of life without despair.

It was this trait of God's character that led the psalmist David to say, "I wait quietly before God, for my victory comes from him. He alone is my rock and my salvation, my fortress where I will never be shaken" (Psalm 62:1-2). The same David wrote, on another occasion: "My God, my God, why have you abandoned me? Why are you so far away when I groan for help?" (Psalm 22:1). We can talk to God just as we are, without being rejected despite our present weakness. Praise God, who doesn't always answer us when and how we want! When he denies us our desired answers, in our desired way, he gives us what we did not know to ask for, but which will satisfy our soul.

Are we the only ones who have moments of questioning, despair, or misperceptions about how God acts and works in our lives and in the world? And in such moments, how should we act?

Jesus, Habakkuk and us

In waiting rooms, we suffer from helplessness and abandonment. Loneliness becomes our companion. It is in these circumstances that we discover that, in spite of everything, we can experience an important, profound, and unique moment where we can be alone with Christ.

It was on the cross of Calvary in the midst of the pain of his separation from the one who had sent him to earth, that Jesus turned to the Father and, quoting Psalm 22, said, "My God, my God, why have you abandoned me?" (Matthew 27:46). Jesus did not deny his emotions while anguish was tearing his whole being apart. But this was the path he had chosen. And it is precisely because he died on the cross and experienced the anguish of loneliness that Jesus understands us. Our Savior is able to help us in the midst of despair and loneliness, and we must remember this. The fruit of grace is being able to run to Jesus in our hours of anguish, being able to talk to the Father about what is going on in our hearts and question Him freely without suffering rejection. This is the grace that was given to us through Jesus Christ.

Pedro and Dora were still in the waiting room when the doctor finally appeared. The couple looked at him with hope, but he said, "I am sorry, your son has suffered a neurological problem that needs more attention and perhaps we will need to transfer him to another hospital. Go home and as soon as we have better news, we will call you. For now, just wait." At that moment, the couple realized that they would remain in the waiting room for some time.

Our trust in Jesus in times of despair is based on who he is and what he does and has done for us.

So then, since we have a great High Priest who has entered heaven, Jesus the Son of God, let us hold firmly to what we believe. This High Priest of ours understands our weaknesses, for he faced all of the same testings we do, yet he did not sin. So let us come boldly to the throne of our gracious God. There we will receive his mercy, and we will find grace to help us when we need it most.

Hebrews 4:14-16

Because we are sinners, we do not deserve this access to God. But Jesus died on the cross not only to forgive our sins, but also to open the way for us to reach God when we our souls are dilacerated. We cannot survive without this grace.

Habakkuk did not use the language of Hebrews 4:14-16, but he did put its teaching into practice. He approached the throne of grace with confidence. The prophet saw his people's chaotic situation and did not run away; instead, he admitted the emotions, the anguish, and the pain he was experiencing. And he went even further. He questioned God, prayed, and opened his heart. In the process, instead of receiving the answer he expected, he heard that the situation of his people would get worse. And how did he respond? He continued to stand before God, and thus discovered a God who is holy, welcoming, and loving, and who generates stability and security. *In order to maintain an emotional and rational balance in the waiting room, we must stand before God and open up our hearts to Him.*

Because of Jesus, we can also have the same experience and open our hearts to a God who welcomes us even when we vent foolish thoughts, stemming from our mistaken perception of him. Paraphrasing one of John Piper's expressions, "we cannot waste our sorrows."[7] In the midst of them, we discover that God leads us from despair to hope. Habakkuk felt abandoned, but instead of nursing the feeling of abandonment, he ran to God, his Rock. Instead of focusing on unanswered questions, he expressed his feelings by focusing on the holy God who does not lie.

> In order to maintain an emotional and rational balance in the waiting room, we must stand before God and open up our hearts to Him.

We need to remember that the God who sent his Son to die for us when we deserved eternal punishment is always working to do something exceptional in our lives, even when we don't understand his actions. We are not called to understand everything God does. We are called to know, love, and obey him.

Waiting for news from the doctor when my wife was in labor was a harrowing experience. Would my child survive? Would Teca survive? I saw the nurse walk by with a baby and wondered if it was my son. After awhile the neonatologist called me aside and said, "Your child probably won't survive. You can watch the nurse taking care of him through the glass of the ICU window, but he probably won't hold on much longer." I was in a distressing waiting room for a long time and didn't know how I would get out. I had a lot of questions, but I also had a patient God who tolerated my questions and who was doing a wonderful work in my life and that of my family.

It is at this point that we discover the God who takes us from despair to hope, walking step by step with us on this long journey. How do we understand this God, who is loving, powerful, and our Rock, but who acts as he does? How do we live with this sovereign God, from whose control nothing escapes but whose plans often include leaving us in a waiting room? That's what we'll consider in the next chapter.

In the Waiting Room with a Sovereign God

Does God really control all things?

When we leave home, we are not sure if or how we will return. This was the experience of Joubert's family. The 23-year-old left home around 6 a.m. for the four-hour drive to his state capital. It was a customary journey which would become very memorable.

After finishing college, Joubert was accepted to study for a master's degree in theology at one of the most prestigious seminaries in the country. Since he was 17, he had believed God's plan for his life was to go to the mission field. Completing his higher education was the first stage. While he continued his studies, he could work as an independent professional and open a business that would benefit the community and use his profession as an evangelistic channel to train leaders for local churches. His family was in total agreement with these plans and understood that, in a few years, Joubert would no longer be with them.

But during that trip, everything changed. At around 7 o'clock, a drunk driver in an oncoming vehicle collided with Joubert's car. He was admitted to the hospital in critical condition. His parents were stunned by the news. During the two-hour trip to the hospital, they cried and prayed and asked themselves why God had let this happen to such a good young man who was so devoted to God and eager to serve him. Could it be that the mission field was not God's will for Joubert and that he was preventing him from proceeding with those plans? How could the Lord have let this happen to them when they had always been so faithful to him and devoted to raising their children according to the Gospel of Christ?

They arrived at the hospital at the same time as their family pastor. Between hugs and prayers, the pastor told them: "God is sovereign and has plans for Joubert." They listened to him, but couldn't help asking themselves: "Is God really sovereign?," "Does God really have control over everything that happens to us?," and "If God is both sovereign and loving, couldn't he have stopped that driver from drinking or swerved his car to avoid the collision?".

Joubert's parents had known Christ for many years, but the pain of seeing their son who had been planning to go to the mission field suffer in this way left them bewildered. Dealing with the issue of God's sovereignty was especially hard for them. They begrudgingly nodded along with the pastor's words.

Habakkuk was also stunned when he heard that the Lord would use the Babylonians to punish God's people. How could he reconcile the loving and protective side of God with this punitive side? How could he harmonize the status of God's people with the divine decision to use an impious people as an instrument of punishment? How could he live with a God he knew was sovereign, but whose sovereignty didn't seem to make sense at the time and appeared to be inconsistent with the Lord's character?

Joubert's parents experienced the same conflict. They had tried to live right before God, and yet the pain caught up with them. Now what? How could Habakkuk and Joubert's parents deal with the situation and the reality of God's sovereignty? What if the Babylonians exterminated the Jews? What if Joubert died or became paraplegic? And what about you and me? *What happens when we are faced with the dilemma of believing in God's sovereignty despite desperate situations, fear for the future, and the adverse results of a catastrophe?* Is God really in control of the future? Or do we have a share in God's sovereignty?

> What happens when we are faced with the dilemma of believing in God's sovereignty despite desperate situations, fear for the future, and the adverse results of a catastrophe?

We live in a culture of relief. Anti-anxiety medications are readily available to assuage anxiety and to allow us to sleep and rest. To help us deal with helplessness in facing life's pressures, there are synthetic drugs that lead users into a falsely secure cave. For the afflictions that need to be faced with spiritual resources, there are false teachings, which promise that God does not want us to suffer, does not want us to be poor, and ultimately does not want us to be the tail, but rather the head.

In modern times, Christ's genuine gospel that foresees both good and bad days, has been replaced by a triumphalist gospel in which we create a god in our own image rather than as he truly is, "distorting the true gospel into what might be called goodenough Christianity and denying any call to **radical** discipleship."[1] Radical discipleship implies imitating

Jesus and in doing so, we cannot exempt ourselves from trials, temptations, disappointments, and suffering, for Jesus endured all of these.

Christ did not say that our lives would be triumphalist. On the contrary, he clearly said in bold letters: "Here on earth you will have many trials and sorrows" (John 16:33). Jesus never guaranteed us a life without loss, pain, disappointment, divorce, drug-addicted children, pornography-addicted spouses, cancer, or homosexual relatives. Jesus never said that believers would not have children with genetic problems or degenerative diseases. Nor did he guarantee that we would never be in automobile accidents. On the contrary, he made it clear that in this world we would have afflictions. Some would be the resu1lt of our own decisions; others would be due to the mistakes of other people, as in Joubert's case. Yet none of them are beyond God's control.

One thing is certain. Although God has not guaranteed us freedom from trouble, he has promised to always be there for us. And we must believe in his sovereignty in order to enjoy his presence.

We also experience distressing circumstances arising from God's own decisions, or ones that he allows. Abraham certainly experienced tremendous distress as he climbed Mount Moriah to sacrifice Isaac. Joseph, too, was distressed when he heard his brothers plotting to sell him into slavery. Likewise, Habakkuk's affliction was the result of God's decision to send the Babylonians against Israel to punish the nation for its sins. The same is true for us. If, for example, we run a red light and have a collision, we bear the fruit of our recklessness.

In short, we must always remember that at no time in history has God guaranteed us a life free of problems, challenges, or pain. Many of our internal conflicts with God are due to our thinking that because we are the object of his love, we will be free from problems or that they will be resolved in the way we expect and in the time we desire.

We also think that if we live a righteous life, God is obligated to reward us with good things and deliver us from all evil, keeping us from losing our jobs or getting sick. Because of these misconceptions, we often twist God's words to fit what we imagine.

Nevertheless, bad news can often become good news in God's hands. But if we do not keep in mind that God has not just promised us healthy, happy days as followers of Jesus, we will not always take bad news as good. The biblical message even says that if we want to live a life of devotion to Christ, we will suffer persecution (2 Timothy 3:12).

When we begin to follow Christ, we experience unimaginable conflicts. By choosing to follow him, we will experience difficult things that are either imposed on us or are a result of our choices. Among these difficulties is the dilemma of recognizing God's sovereignty and deciding to accept afflictions or to rebel against them. At this crossroads, we must choose between trusting God or running away from him. If we run away, we are giving up the belief that even on bad days or in the midst of adverse circumstances, he is always there with us.

How can we understand God in situations where afflictions don't seem to make sense or are not a result of our own mistakes? And when they are not the fruit of our errors, how can we keep from despairing? One thing is certain. Although God has not guaranteed us freedom from trouble, he has promised to always be there for us. And we must believe in his sovereignty in order to enjoy his presence.

God is sovereign every day

Habakkuk was struggling with the fact that God used the Babylonians to punish Israel. Although the prophet accepted God disciplining his people for their sins, it was hard for him to see the Babylonians' involvement given their moral profile. Jonah felt the same way when God acted on behalf of the Ninevites. And it was hard for Joubert's parents to accept God's sovereignty knowing he could have prevented their son's accident. In Habakkuk's day the kingdom of Judah had not yet been overrun by the Babylonians. However, some seven decades earlier God had announced to another prophet, Isaiah, the fall of Babylon itself. These are the words of the Lord concerning his sovereignty, recorded in the book of Isaiah:

> Remember the things I have done in the past.
> For I alone am God!
> I am God, and there is none like me.
> Only I can tell you the future before it even happens.
> Everything I plan will come to pass,
> for I do whatever I wish.
> I will call a swift bird of prey from the east—
> a leader from a distant land to come and do my bidding.
> I have said what I would do,
> and I will do it.
>
> Isaiah 46:9-11

This text is a treatise on the sovereignty of God, which we need to accept in order to deal with the catastrophes and waiting rooms of life. The prophecy mentioned in the book of Isaiah shows that God has control of the present and the future. He not only knows what will happen, but he determines and brings about everything he has planned: "I have said what I would do, and I will do it."

In dealing with God's sovereignty, we comprehend something unique. God does not just say what will happen and then distance himself from the world. Rather, he engages in the fulfillment of what he has determined. Therefore, we are comforted by the fact that nothing that happens to us personally nor collectively is beyond the Lord's control. And because God is sovereign, nothing I do changes the path he has set. The Lord said: "Everything I plan will come to pass, for I do whatever I wish." In his book *Truths That Transform*, James Kennedy refers to the sovereignty of God as follows: "There is no man or group of men capable of opposing, thwarting, or limiting any of God's purposes."[2]

Clearly the Lord's plans for Joubert's life were not altered because of the accident. If we trust in an all-seeing, all-controlling, sovereign God, we feel safe.

Habakkuk regarded the divine plans carried out by the Babylonians as vile and incoherent. But in truth, the Lord in his sovereignty is free to determine the future and to choose the means of bringing it about. And since he is God, naturally the path he determines is better than the one I would choose. The paths we choose are usually based on our constant well-being, without pain, suffering, or any need to face life's harsh realities. That's why being in the waiting room is so painful. Yet God's paths always glorify him and benefit us, for he is interested in forming, pruning, shaping, and building us up. God wants us to be like Jesus, whose path included loss, pain, rejection, and Calvary. Why should it be any different for us? Divine sovereignty is clear when we look at the difficult moments experienced by biblical characters such as Joseph, Samson, and Stephen, and when we observe some of God's acts in nature.

> He sends his orders to the world—
> how swiftly his word flies!
> He sends the snow like white wool;
> he scatters frost upon the ground like ashes.
> He hurls the hail like stones.
> Who can stand against his freezing cold?
> Then, at his command, it all melts.
> He sends his winds, and the ice thaws.
>
> Psalm 147:15-18

Reading this psalm makes it impossible to escape the reality that God is involved in what happens in nature; he causes, controls, and sustains it. As Jerry Bridges wrote in his book, *Is God Really in Control?*: "God has not walked away from the day-to-day control of His creation. Certainly He has established physical laws by which He governs the forces of nature, but those laws continuously operate according to His sovereign will."[3]

> God's ways always glorify him and benefit us, for he is interested in forming, pruning, shaping, and building us up.

The God who can hurl hail can also stop a flood or halt a tsunami. The God who sends cold weather has the power to cause a storm, such as the one the disciples faced on the Sea of Galilee (Mark 4:35-41). We may doubt this truth when someone we love loses a house in a storm or a child in an airplane crash due to an uncontrollable windstorm. But we need to trust that the God who did not stop the storm is the God who knows all things and is in total control.

We do not have complete answers as to why God allows such things. Nor can we fully understand why he did not prevent certain disasters from happening, knowing that many people would perish, as in the case of hurricanes and tsunamis. By contrast, as Bridges tells us, "We must be careful not to, in our minds, take God off his throne of absolute sovereignty or put him in the dock and bring him to the bar of our judgement." [4]

Thus, Jesus's teaching is not figurative when he says: "What is the price of two sparrows—one copper coin? But not a single sparrow can fall to the ground without your Father knowing it. And the very hairs on your head are all numbered" (Matthew 10:29-30). If the Lord has control over the lives of sparrows and knows how many hairs we have, wouldn't we be a part of his purposes? If God controls the existence of the sparrows, doesn't he have control over our lives? Jesus tells us to "look at the birds. They don't plant or harvest or store food in barns, for your heavenly Father feeds them. And aren't you far more valuable to him than they are?" (Matthew 6:26). Christ's statements lead us to believe that God has control over everything, from the galaxies to the atoms of all matter. Likewise, he has control and power over what happens around us and to those we love.

This does not mean, however, that God approves or causes everything that happens, in any and every context. Having sovereignty over everything does not mean that the Lord causes an assassination or pretends not to see corruption in the heart of a high government official. What we mean by sovereignty is that ultimately the Lord has power over everything, including whether or not to prevent criminal action.

God's power can function as a causative agent or as a permissive agent. In the context of the book of Habakkuk, the Lord saw his people's moral and religious corruption. Could he have prevented it? Of course. But he chose to put an end to the nation's rampant sin and at the same time discipline them through the Babylonians, whose violence, immorality, and power were no surprise to God. Allowing the Babylonians to invade Judah was a divine and sovereign decision. We need to believe that when the Lord does not prevent something bad or makes decisions contrary to what we expect, it is because he is in control and sees the best plan for our lives, even if today we think it is the worst.

> We need to believe that when the Lord does not prevent something bad or makes decisions contrary to what we expect, it is because he is in control and sees the best plan for our lives, even if today we think it is the worst.

It was as inexplicable to Habakkuk that God would use the Babylonians as it was to Joubert's parents to see their son in intensive care, knowing that he had dedicated his life to the Lord. When we have difficulty accepting God's sovereignty and what happens to us by his permission, we can doubt the Lord's love. The reality is that we consider God's sovereignty good only when his difficult acts bless us according to our understanding of what a blessing is and who God is. But we cannot define the Lord's sovereignty and character based on our own understanding. We need to consider them according to what is written in the Word. Divine sovereignty gives the Lord the freedom to make whatever choices he wishes about what does or does not affect our lives. In exercising his sovereign will, God glorifies himself and, in doing so, does not harm people, even if it appears that way.

Being sovereign, God told Abraham that his descendants would be slaves for 400 years in Egypt and then be freed. The Almighty's aim was to form a people resilient to suffering, which is a blessing. By allowing Joseph to be taken into slavery in Egypt, God was fulfilling the promises he had made centuries earlier to Abraham, preserving his people, exalting Joseph, and being glorified. In the heat of the moment, this reality was not apparent, but today, seeing the bigger picture, we clearly perceive the divine action.

In our lives, as in the lives of Habakkuk, Joseph, Abraham, and Joubert, God always acts in a sovereignly loving way. He wants to lead his beloved ones from despair to hope, even if we remain for long periods in waiting rooms, where the Lord is with us.

God is always good

Habakkuk was used to seeing God's actions on good days. It is important to remember the Lord's love when we prosper in business, feel loved and important in marriage, or see our children progress at school. God is always good, and these joyful phases of life remind us of that. However, we must not allow this realization to fade away in the days of hardship or scarcity. God is always good, during the days when we have been protected from catastrophe and also in those when catastrophe strikes.

It is always crucial to see God's sovereignty alongside his love. For example, let's compare Habakkuk's experience with the divine truth the apostle Paul affirms in Romans:

> And we know that God causes everything to work together for the good of those who love God and are called according to his purpose for them. For God knew his people in advance, and he chose them to become like his Son, so that his Son would be the firstborn among many brothers and sisters. And having chosen them, he called them to come to him. And having called them, he gave them right standing with himself. And having given them right standing, he gave them his glory.
>
> Romans 8:28-30

If we believe that these words are true and that all truth comes from God, we must consider evil circumstances in the light of this understanding. We are often blinded by our haste in trying to understand God's ways, when in reality he has not yet finished revealing them. As a result, we are slow to understand how all things work together for our good, especially those things that bring pain, loss, or suffering. This can cause us to question God's goodness.

We must remember that things do not always happen automatically. God plans and determines, but he likes to involve people and give them responsibility in the equation. For example, when we think of the crucifixion of Jesus, we see that the cross was the way set forth by the Trinity for the redemption of humanity. Even so, God did not exclude human responsibility, as the apostle Peter clearly states:

> People of Israel, listen! God publicly endorsed Jesus the Nazarene by doing powerful miracles, wonders, and signs through

him, as you well know. But God knew what would happen, and his prearranged plan was carried out when Jesus was betrayed. With the help of lawless Gentiles, you nailed him to a cross and killed him.

Acts 2:22-23

Jesus was crucified according to God's predetermined plan, but Peter shows that men were also responsible. Men nailed Jesus to the cross, which was only possible as a result of God's permission, so in this same text God's sovereignty and human responsibility both are evident. How the actions of each overlap or interact is beyond complete human comprehension.

This co-participation takes place not only in difficult or sinful situations, but also in those which appear positive from the outset. For example, God said he would not abandon his chosen people, but at the same time he would not let sin persist in the nation. Despite the Israelites' disobedience, God would not let their behavior hinder his plans and they would be punished if they persevered in it. Although the Lord was punishing the nation through Babylon, he was not abandoning them or forsaking his plans to be their only God. In some cases, God's sovereignty includes discipline, but not discipline for destruction, but for fear and restoration.

When they heard the pastor say that God was sovereign, Joubert's parents felt a certain sense of God's abandonment and a feeling of helplessness in the face of an all-powerful and loving God who "wasn't able" to prevent the accident from happening to their beloved son. Following the same line of reasoning, Habakkuk was going through the process of discovering that God's sovereignty included control over all things, but this control did not mean abandoning His plans. God had not left his people to their own devices. He would use the Babylonians, but they would be under his strict control.

God's sovereignty and character give us security. The apostle Paul uses the same context to tell us that God causes everything to work together for the good of those who love him and that nothing can separate us from his love. Romans 8:31-39 lists the spiritual, material, physical, and temporal circumstances which will not separate us from God's love. This does not mean, however, that we are exempt from trouble, adversity, persecution, hunger, misery, danger, death threats, fears and worries, or the powers of hell. God has not promised us freedom from afflictions. He has promised us that he will not abandon us in any of these circumstances. God promises that by having ultimate control over all things, he makes them work together for our good.

> God has not promised us freedom from afflictions. He has promised us that he will not abandon us in any of these circumstances.

When our son's doctor told me to stay in the waiting room outside the children's ICU, I was overwhelmed with questions. God had reserved many long, lonely hours of waiting for me so that in other circumstances, when I felt helpless, I would know I could trust him. I didn't fully learn then, and I'm still learning, but in his sovereignty he was preparing me for the future.

The God whose actions we don't immediately understand

Habakkuk expressed his feelings to God, and the response was unusual. The prophet did not know Romans 8:28-29, but he knew the compassionate and merciful God. Because of this, the mood of his first chapter moves toward a peaceful resolution.

The sovereign God controls all things and in the end they will work together for our good. This *good* concerns the divine purpose of molding us into the likeness of Christ. Thus, the good that God will provide will not always be an immediate relief or solution to a problem we present to him; it will be that which will bring glory to him and benefit his children.

When Jesus cured the blind Bartimaeus, the man shouted, "Jesus, Son of David, have mercy on me!" (Mark 10:47). The crowd asked him to be quiet, but the Master heard his cry and sent for him. The blind man was worried about his blindness, but Jesus gave him something more than his sight. The blind man asked for the ability to see, but Jesus said: "Go, for your faith has healed you" (Mark 10:52). The verb Mark uses assures us that Jesus not only healed Bartimaeus's physical blindness, but saved him, giving him eternal life.[5] No one would call Jesus the "Son of David" if they did not know 2 Samuel 7:1-17.[6]

God could have prevented Bartimaeus's blindness, but he already knew what Jesus would do later on in that man's life. And if Bartimaeus had been blinded because of a sin he committed, as was the belief of the time, God had already predestined his encounter with Jesus, as well as his physical and spiritual healing. Nothing could separate Bartimaeus from the love God felt for him.

We must not forget that Jesus himself lived in a waiting room, but while there he experienced the deep love of the Father. Before the foundation of the world, Jesus knew what would happen between nine o'clock in the morning and three o'clock in the afternoon on that Friday. Jesus's waiting room pain began thousands of years earlier and deepened from the day of his baptism when his persecution began. As a human, he waited for those thirty years that culminated in his crucifixion. In the early hours of the day when he would suffer at the hands of his executioners, Jesus pleaded uselessly with the Father for relief from his suffering, but the Son knew his Father. And though he trusted the sovereign Father, his human side asked if he could possibly be released from the cup of his passion.

Imagine what would have happened if the Father had answered Jesus's prayer! None of us would have eternal life! For this greater good, Jesus accepted the Father's will as his deepest worship of God and deepest expression of love for us. As the apostle Paul wrote: "What shall we say about such wonderful things as these? If God is for us, who can ever be against us? Since he did not spare even his own Son but gave him up for us all, won't he also give us everything else?" (Romans 8:31-32).

God will give us all the circumstances, experiences, and resources necessary to produce the character of Christ in us. Having Jesus's nature will satisfy us. In him, we will be satisfied in the face of the unusual, the unknown, the strange, and the impossible to experience with human resources. But this is possible only as a result of God's love for us and the forgiveness of our sins through Christ.

Jesus faced a lonely, cold, and painful waiting room. Above all, he suffered the pain of the Father's rejection, even for just a few moments. All out of love for us. And because of the Father's love for him, Jesus rose again, glorified. Thus, we have someone to run to when we are surrounded by situations we don't understand or thought we would never face.

We cannot risk thinking that because we are God's children we will not experience dark times. Car crashes, babies with disabilities, incomprehensible divorces, drug-addicted children, workplace injustice, premature deaths, and corrupt people being used to punish even people of integrity are all issues that, however incomprehensible they may be, have not escaped God's control. And Habakkuk's God goes on to say that, however incomprehensible his actions, he is doing something extraordinary that will bring glory to him and benefit to us.

When God told Habakkuk that he would do something remarkable, it seemed inconceivable to the prophet that it would be accomplished through the Babylonians. This extraordinary work would only be explained centuries later by Paul and Barnabas in Antioch of Psidia (Acts 13:41). In explaining the coming of Jesus, who he was, and God's purposes through him, the two quote Habakkuk 1:5. They link Old Testament prophecy to the marvelous work of the forgiveness of sins through Christ. What had been obscure to the prophet would become not only God's warning for people to turn back to him, but ultimately it was the complete fulfillment of God's words that would only take place at the coming of the Messiah. It was the culmination of the revelation of the Lord's love for the nation of Israel and the world.

How Habakkuk dealt with the unexpected is what Joubert's parents would need to do. It is also what we all need to do when God's sovereign decisions don't seem to make sense to us. After boldly and personally expressing his frustrations to God, Habakkuk still called him "my Holy One" and "my Rock," and makes a decision that reveals a resigned and trusting heart.

After hours of surgery, the doctor finally opened the door and spoke to Joubert's parents. Before he could even get words out, his parents asked: "Is our son okay? Will he survive?" The doctor replied, "The accident was serious and it was a delicate and time-consuming surgery. Now, we must wait to know the outcome. He may lose the movement of his lower limbs, but we must wait to be sure."

Joubert's parents had the same God as Habakkuk. Shouldn't they have had the same mindset as the prophet's? But how can you have that perspective when you are so weakened and impacted by circumstances? Habakkuk, reconciled and confident, withdrew: "I will climb up to my watchtower and stand at my guardpost. There I will wait to see what the LORD says and how he will answer my complaint" (Habakkuk 2:1).

That tower was his waiting room. There Habakkuk waited for God to work in his life, to take him from despair to hope. When we spend time with God in waiting rooms, we learn that, in his time, the Lord turns years of waiting into periods of satisfaction in him, despite the losses. The end of the first chapter of Habakkuk and the beginning of the second challenge us to do the same. Running to God and being in the waiting room with him is the divine way forward.

The Lord always wishes go beyond what we can even imagine, beyond just relieving our pain. God wants to call us to something deeper than what we are seeing and experiencing. He will always do something marvelous and admirable.

3

Alone but Accompanied by God in the Waiting Room

Does our faith grow or wither while we wait?

After three years of marriage to Joash, Celina began to feel that her husband was no longer interested in her sexually. That playful, affectionate guy from their dating years seemed to have disappeared. Gradually, the couple also stopped getting involved with church activities, and Celina realized that their devotional life was dying. A planned second honeymoon turned into a cold, dull trip with few meaningful conversations. Celina tried to deepen her prayer life, but nothing seemed to change.

One day, what Celina had suspected happened. Saying that he had to leave early for work, Joash left the house quickly. When Celina got up, she found a letter addressed to her on the bedside table. In a few words, Joash wrote: "There was no way to continue hiding or resisting. As much as I loved you, today my heart belongs to someone else and I am leaving home to live with him. Forgive me." In a state of shock, Celina read and reread the passage "leaving home to live with him." Was it really "with him" or "with her"?

Joash's phone was switched off. Celina called her closest friends. Tearfully and in bitterness she asked them, "How could Joash do this to me? Was our marriage a sham? Where is God in all this?" Her friends told her to pray, to keep calm, and to wait on God, because he has a purpose for everything.

When Habakkuk heard that God would use the Babylonians to punish the people of Judah, he said to himself: "I would never expect this from God, how can he do this to me and the people he claims to love?" At different levels and in different contexts, both Habakkuk's experience and the story of Joash and Celina are repeated in many families. There are parents who receive the news that a child has HIV, a mother who discovers that the baby in her womb has some malformation, or a young professional who suffers an accident and has his hand amputated. Frustrations and sudden changes of plans happen without warning. How do you survive situations like these?

When Habakkuk decides to go up to the watchtower to wait for God's answer, the prophet decides meaningfully to give rest to his soul. Climbing the watchtower meant admitting his own helplessness to deal with pains, questions, and predicaments. When we admit our helplessness, we are opening our soul to use divine resources to get through the chaos.

By climbing our watchtower, we are not using the last resort, but putting into practice the greatest and most singular action we are capable of. Retreating to pray remains the most powerful resource God has given us, especially when the tsunami engulfing us is greater than our individual strength.

Waiting for the Lord's answer in waiting rooms is moving from knowing him only intellectually to connecting with him emotionally and spiritually. Habakkuk's life seemed to be on pause. Celina felt the same way. Habakkuk made the right decision, but Celina was still in shock. The fact is that sooner or later, as the fruit of his grace, the Father will meet us in waiting rooms in order to demonstrate his love.

"Waiting on the Lord" is one of the most common concepts in God's Word. Practicing this discipline destroys our immediate tendency to want to be in control of everything. It is difficult to wait on the Lord, but it's worse to try to be like God and thus try to control something that is beyond our capacity. So Habakkuk's decision to run to his waiting room was the wisest possible solution. Shouldn't we do the same?

The verb in Hebrew that Habakkuk uses has been translated as "to wait."[1] It carries a particular meaning for the context in which he was living. It means to look attentively, to peer, to observe the situation like a sentinel in a watchtower who, upon noticing a strange movement, remains vigilant to understand what is happening and intervene if necessary. So Habakkuk's decision to wait meant that he would watch for God to act.

> When we admit our helplessness, we are opening our soul to use divine resources to get through the chaos.

Thus, it is not a passive or resigned stance. We cannot go to the waiting room suspecting that God has left the scene, and simply accept the situation as if nothing more can be done. On the contrary, our attitude must be like that of the farmer who, in times of drought, constantly looks to the horizon with the certainty that, sooner or later, the rain will come. To hope in God is not to be passive. It is to live in expectation, attentive to what God will do and with the certainty that the Lord, although he may seem silent, is actually on the move, acting out of sight. So when we run to the waiting room, we can have the confidence that we will surely find the Almighty there. This understanding removes all of our anxiety, because instead of focusing on the problem, we focus on the person of God.

Remember that his love for us does not change, even though our love for him may falter because we fail to understand what he is doing at any given time.

Time, hope, and patience

A watchtower was the place where sentries stood to perform their duties. The Psalms say: "I am counting on the LORD; yes, I am counting on him. I have put my hope in his word. I long for the LORD more than sentries long for the dawn, yes, more than sentries long for the dawn" (Psalm 130:5-6). We see here both the concept of waiting on the Lord and that of hope. Our waiting for God should be similar to the sentinels's waiting for the dawn. They don't have a watch, but they are sure that the sun will rise and the day will dawn.

If we do not know God's character, we can only guess what God can or will do for us. But if we know and trust that he is sovereign and that nothing escapes his control and that nothing separates us from his love, no matter how uncontrollable the storm, we can rest in the assurance that at the right time he will intervene. "There I will wait to see what the LORD says." Hope becomes certainty.

In addition to the concepts of time and hope, Habakkuk's decision to wait on God includes the idea of patience. After sowing his field, a farmer must wait without giving up. He would perhaps like the fruit to appear the next day, but he must be patient and submit to the processes that God has created for the proper functioning of nature. Thus, instead of fighting with nature or even cursing it for the delay, it would be healthier for the farmer to humbly submit to the processes of the law of agriculture.

We should have the same attitude when God places us or allows us to sit in a waiting room. Humility is a key word for the exercise of patience. Humility carries the meaning of accepting what a superior asks us to be or do, even when we do not understand what motivates his request. We are humble when we accept that we submit to God's will and processes even though we do not understand them. We are humble when we recognize our inability or helplessness to deal with a situation and accept the fact that God is in control. And because we believe this, we do not lose hope, nor does time become a source of anxiety. We wait patiently.

God uses time to produce pearls in us. We would be arrogant to tell him that he is taking too long. Can you imagine a pearl saying to the Creator: "Please hurry up, I can't take it anymore!" And God's reply might be: "All right, but if I hurry the process, you won't be as valuable or beautiful." The patience of Job the patriarch is clear from his words: "When he tests me, I will come out as pure as gold" (Job 23:10). This statement shows both the certainty of divine action and the acceptance of God's timing.

God uses disappointments and losses to teach us. It was devastating for Job to lose his possessions. And even more overwhelming was burying his children. Is there any pain worse for a parent than to bury a child? Yet Job's attitude was not to blame God (Job 1:22). Instead, he humbly and patiently waited for divine intervention, not knowing when it would occur.

Humility, then, means accepting the Lord's processes by submitting to them by faith. While "accepting" alone can communicate passivity or resignation, "accepting by submitting" communicates proactivity to remain in God's ways. And because of our humility, the Holy Spirit helps us develop patience, which is one of the virtues of the fruit of the Spirit (Galatians 5:22).

Humility also makes us feel like we are losing control. As we surrender control of the situation into God's hands, we allow him to take the necessary time to act in our lives, using circumstances to fulfill His purposes. At that point, divine patience can develop within us.

God was doing a marvelous work among his people and in the life of Habakkuk (Habakkuk 1:5-6). When we place

> We will go through the pain of loss, but we will find that putting our focus on God and meeting him in the waiting room will have an eternal impact that we would never experience elsewhere.

time, hope, and patience at the feet of Jesus, it is as if we are saying to God: "We don't understand anything. We are suffering, but we give ourselves to your care and we will wait for what you are going to tell us." This is what Habakkuk did when he decided to go up to the watchtower and wait there for the divine answer to his complaints.

Celina wasn't ready to experience this reality. Joash had only recently left her. She did not have the power to bring him back, nor to turn him into a heterosexual man. She didn't know how God was working in her husband's life, so the only course of action for that moment was to admit that she was in a waiting room and needed to go up to the watchtower. The thing is, this doesn't always happen quickly. As it was with Habakkuk, there is a process to heed.

I received a phone call from a dear family: "Lisânias, my father has had a heart attack and is on his way to the hospital. Please pray, we won't know how to live without him." Is this true? We cannot live without the person we love the most? *We will go through the pain of loss, but we will find that putting our focus on God and meeting him in the waiting room will have an eternal impact that we would never experience elsewhere.*

I believe Celina's attitude should be the same as Habakkuk's. It is the same one we should have when we get a cancer diagnosis, when a glorious career comes to an end, or when a teenage daughter tells her parents she's pregnant. Time, hope, and humility are all present while "waiting in the watchtower."

Our attitudes in the waiting room

We do not have the power nor the control to escape the unexpected that takes us to where it is hard to wait. After 25 years in pastoral ministry, I know almost every hospital waiting room in São Paulo, as well as most of the ICUs in our city. My wife and I have walked alongside dear brothers and sisters in moments of pain and despair. But we have also experienced the joy of growing alongside several others who have lived prolonged times in their waiting rooms, not only in hospitals, but at home, while waiting for God's intervention in their story. In each case, it was clear that the attitude one takes in each circumstance contributes profoundly to making the time in these rooms fruitful and the experience with God meaningful.

Habakkuk talked to the Lord about what he was feeling. In these conversations, he built a relationship with God that was unprecedented in his life. Speaking with the Lord soothes the soul, connects us more deeply with him, and moves us forward on our journey with him. The prophet decided to wait on God, but he also made other decisions that comprised a unique and meaningful scenario, making his time in the waiting room a period marked with the Almighty's grace. From his watchtower, Habakkuk did not focus on the problem, but on what the Lord wanted to tell him and accomplish in his life.

In our watchtower, we need to look at problems from a divine perspective. I remember the first time I went to the Ipiranga Museum in São Paulo. I was delighted when I saw the fantastic painting by Pedro Américo entitled "Independence or Death," which depicts the proclamation of Brazil's independence I was thrilled when, from a longer distance, I could see significant details of this great Brazilian artist's work. The distance allowed me to have a much broader perspective of the whole, which would have been imperceptible from up close.

Seeing circumstances from the divine perspective is crucial if we are to grow in the waiting room and enjoy God's presence and love as he desires to reveal himself to us. This is how the apostle Paul encouraged us to see circumstances when he references Isaiah 64:4: "No eye has seen, no ear has heard, and no mind has imagined what God has prepared for those who love him" (1 Corinthians 2:9). Habakkuk did not have a clear understanding of the divine processes, but he made the right decision to go up to the watchtower and watch for what God would do. If God chose us before the foundation of the world to be holy and blameless before him, if he predestined us for adoption as sons, would his work in us be done? Would he abandon us to our own fate? Certainly not.

Thus, seeing circumstances from a divine perspective implies believing that God is at work in the process I am experiencing. The outcome is beyond our imagination. When the people of Israel found themselves trapped between the Red Sea and Pharaoh's army, the feeling was one of despair. But God used that seemingly unsolvable circumstance to show the people his power. The Lord had a way out that the Israelites would have never considered. In fact, he was preparing something that ears have never heard and eyes have never seen.

When Joseph, son of Jacob, learned from inside a well that his brothers would sell him into slavery, he could not imagine the beautiful things God was planning for his life. What the Lord was preparing was difficult to see at that moment, but his love was present in everything. The well was not the end of Joseph's life. Instead, he was taken from the bottom of the pit to a top position in Pharaoh's court. It took many years, but God did not forget Joseph. Time, patience, and hope were part of his story.

> The Lord had a way out that the Israelites would have never considered. In fact, he was preparing something that ears have never heard and eyes have never seen.

Likewise, when Jochebed produced a wicker basket and placed baby Moses in it, she was certainly unaware that God was leading her infant son into the hands of the princess of Egypt and that he would deliver the people of Israel. God turned a mother's pain into an experience of grace and love (Exodus 2:1-14). Later, Moses spent forty years in the waiting room of the Midian Desert, where God prepared him to become the greatest leader the nation had ever known. It was in the wilderness, in the long solitude of the waiting room, that Moses was unknowingly being shaped to become the man God wanted him to be (Exodus 2:11-4:29).

Twenty-seven years ago, I fell into depression. Until then, either through lack of knowledge or pride, I believed that depression was the result of some sin. Although this diagnosis greatly affected my pride, it was one of God's processes in my life that most prepared me for the ministry he would lead me to as pastor of the church where I am today. Those were difficult, cloudy, exhausting months, a situation I never want to face again. But God was dealing with something I needed to change in order to move forward with the plans he had for my life. He was accomplishing something in me that my eyes had never seen and my ears had never heard.

When crises, disappointments, and catastrophes hit us, we need time to assimilate them. But eventually we need to decide whether to continue to focus on the problem and question God or to climb the watchtower in an attempt to see the circumstances from God's perspective. The second option involves believing that God not only has purposes for what we do not understand, but that this is part of all he is preparing for us. Joseph did not understand, nor did Jehobel, nor did Moses. But the day came when they experienced something they had never heard, seen, or imagined.

Surely the most natural prayer for Celina would be: "Father, bring my husband back, and as a heterosexual." What Habakkuk wanted was for the Babylonians not to be used by God. But God was planning something beyond that. The divine perspective sees beyond the problem, like a sentinel who does not just focus on the outskirts of the city, but who scans the horizon.

In Habakkuk's situation, which was more important? The people being healed of sin, going through the humiliation of a wicked nation invading their country, or remaining in darkness due to the shame of being disciplined by the Babylonians? Could it be that in Celina's case, the fact that God had allowed Joash's choice might mean that he had a greater purpose in the future.

When we find ourselves in a waiting room, it is unavoidable to think: "Lord, have I done something wrong that you want to show me?" This was also David's question: "Search me, O God, and know my heart; test me and know my anxious thoughts. Point out anything in me that offends you, and lead me along the path of everlasting life" (Psalm 139:23-24). When we seek to regard our difficult circumstances from a divine perspective, "Search me, O God" becomes a courageous prayer.

Habakkuk may not have understood God's chosen process for punishing the nation, but that did not mean that God's wisdom was not at work. We always need to remember that regardless of the reason that brings us to an unbearable waiting room, God is there with us, treating us inwardly and seeking to give us more than just pain relief. As Mike Wells summarizes it so well, God doesn't stop operating just because we don't see what he is doing.[2] Facing sin, recognizing inner idols, and seeing God's processes from a divine perspective are dispositions that help us survive a prolonged or short season in the waiting room.

I like a statement I read in the *On the Journey with Christ* study Bible: "Being a Christian does not exempt us from suffering. You will suffer. Don't let people deceive you by promising you otherwise."[3] It reflects Paul's words about the purpose of his suffering: "Yet what we suffer now is nothing compared to the glory he will reveal to us later" (Romans 8:18). The Greek term, translated "compared," means "to take into account," "to think seriously," "to be fully convinced," "to have a strong opinion" about the subject being discussed.[4]

It means that whether we are facing suffering or in the waiting rooms of life, our attitude needs to be the same. The change in our situation that God is planning for us might come in a few months, but it may take many years. The text from Romans certainly considers what God has in store for us in the future, whether at Jesus's return or in the new heavens and the new earth. We must remember that that life here on earth may last up to 100 years, but what about eternal life with God?

> Facing sin, recognizing inner idols, and seeing God's processes from a divine perspective are dispositions that help us survive a prolonged or short season in the waiting room.

The pains that brought us to the waiting room are infinitesimal compared to what God has prepared for us in eternity.

The waiting room challenges us to persevere and have faith

The watchtower Habakkuk went up had a military function. The watchman was there to warn of impending danger. At his warning, the city or the city's army could begin a mobilization capable of confronting the oncoming enemy.

Habakkuk's phrase, "I will climb up to my watchtower and stand at my guardpost," has a strong military tone. While on the watchtower, the watchman might face cold, heat, boredom, fatigue, disappointment, hunger, danger, or whatever else, but he would never be allowed to abandon his post. Habakkuk was saying that he would take a firm stand, whatever the cost.[5]

When we are under the pressure of painful circumstances for a long time, we get tired and often want to give up. The long wait for divine action and the weariness raise questions such as: "Is it worth it to keep waiting on God?" and then we often stop reading the Bible and praying. We decide to "take a break" from activities such as serving people and getting involved in church ministry. We lose the will to witness, because our faith sounds like fiction and we don't want to be hypocrites. We tend to drift away from fellowship and Bible study groups because we don't have many blessings to tell, only questions and even complaints. And so we miss the opportunity to grow and be comforted by sharing our sorrows with our brothers and sisters.

We cannot deny that prolonged times in the waiting room wear us out and rob us of strength. The apostle Paul went through such times. He was betrayed, persecuted, and shipwrecked; he starved and physically suffered the pains of persecution.

> We serve God whether people honor us or despise us, whether they slander us or praise us. We are honest, but they call us impostors. We are ignored, even though we are well known. We live close to death, but we are still alive. We have been beaten, but we have not been killed. Our hearts ache, but we always have joy. We are poor, but we give spiritual riches to others. We own nothing, and yet we have everything.
>
> 2 Corinthians 6:8-10

Paul describes his feelings and actions during the long periods in the waiting room, but he doesn't give up. In purely human terms, the apostle lost a lot by giving up his former life to devote himself to Christ. That is our challenge too. When we are tempted to give up trust—which is perhaps our greatest challenge under the pressure of time—we need to remember that time belongs to God and that he always has wonderful purposes for our lives, and so it is worth standing guard in the waiting room.

What would Celina be like in her watchtower? Would she stand guard? Would she realize that what God had for her in the near future or in eternity would be so much greater than the pain of being abandoned by her husband? What about you and me? Are we being tempted to give up remaining in the waiting room? Habakkuk has more to show us about how God takes us from despair to hope.

The prophet had gone up to the watchtower to wait for God's answer, and it was not what Habakkuk had expected. Nevertheless, instead of diminishing, his confidence was invigorated, for God did not leave him unanswered. He is sovereignly loving to do what he wills, but he also gives us freedom to pray while we wait for his actions.

Habakkuk didn't show any disappointment. His experience let him know that God would provide the stability he needed. God commands the prophet to write on tablets what he was revealing to him. Even though the fulfillment of the prophecy seemed delayed, his words would come true, and the Babylonians would indeed come. Believing this required faith and faithfulness.

> He is sovereignly loving to do what he wills, but he also gives us freedom to pray while we wait for his actions.

Faith is essential for us to survive prolonged periods in the waiting room. God's language with Habakkuk may seem insensitive, but the Lord was working a marvelous work in his life. God goes on to describe the Babylonians while also discussing what he expects to see in the lives of his people. "'Look at the proud! They trust in themselves, and their lives are crooked. But the righteous will live by their faithfulness to God (Habakkuk 2:4). In other translations of the Bible, we read "the just shall live by faith" (NKJV). What does this mean?

In order to understand living by faith in this context, we need to remember that the prophet knew of God's covenant with Abraham (Genesis 15). The Lord had promised that he would make a great nation of the patriarch's descendants, whose members would be more numerous than the stars in heaven. It was an unconditional promise and, as such, it could not fail. Thus, although the Babylonians would come to punish the nation, this did not mean its annihilation. Certainly, none of this was clear to Habakkuk, but he should have remembered what the prophet Isaiah had said: "'My thoughts are nothing like your thoughts,' says the LORD. 'And my ways are far beyond anything you could imagine'" (Isaiah 55:8).

Our obedience to God cannot be tied to whether or not we understand his actions. Faith and faithfulness mean remaining in obedience simply because we know that the Lord does not change and his promises will be fulfilled! And precisely because God is faithful in his promises, we can be faithful to him and have faith in him. Thus, in the context of Habakkuk 2:4, living by faith means being faithful to God simply for who he is. In the original Hebrew, the idea is of steadfastness, permanence, stability, trust. Faith is not based on feelings or mere superstition. Faith is based on the certainty that the Lord is sovereign to accomplish what he has promised. Because he knew the God who had formed a covenant with his people, Habakkuk could trust his words. Abraham believed what

God said, which made him a righteous man (Romans 4:3). The prophet followed his example.

This righteousness, however, is the result of God's action in Abraham's life, not his own merit. When we choose to believe in Jesus as our sufficient Savior to forgive our sins, we become righteous before God, not by our own merit, but by what Christ has done for us. To have been justified by faith or to live by faith implies acknowledging that on our own we cannot attain the standard of holiness that God desires for our lives, and therefore, we deserve punishment. But Jesus took it upon Himself in our place, and because we believe in him, our punishment has been canceled, and we are forgiven and acquitted.

When we trust in what God says, even in the midst of the catastrophe of chaos, anxiety, and fear, our walk remains faithful to Him, and we will continue to be obedient. Even though we may have moments of questioning, our character will not be compromised. We will continue to do what God desires, despite the internal struggles that press us to doubt His love. What enables a righteous person to navigate through chaos and not despair in the waiting room is the certainty that God is with them, even if they don't feel it. Faith does not imply the absence of fear, but rather the assurance of God's presence and his provision of resources to overcome fear and survive the chaos.

When we were encouraged to abort our second child, occasionally the fear that my wife would die would torment me. But what gave me the strength to make it to the delivery day was knowing that God would sustain us if our child died and that he would sustain me if my wife and child died. The Lord never promised us that we would not have afflictions because we are his children. On the contrary, Jesus assured us that in this world we would have afflictions. But because we are God's children, the Lord loves us unconditionally and he promises to be with us always.

Because of his unchanging character and unconditional love, God encourages us to have an unshakable trust. As Maurício Zágari says in his book *Unshakable Trust,*[6] this is a trust that God calls *faith.*

This is why the author of Hebrews wrote: "'And my righteous ones will live by faith. But I will take no pleasure in anyone who turns away.' But we are not like those who turn away from God to their

> Faith does not imply the absence of fear, but rather the assurance of God's presence and his provision of resources to overcome fear and survive the chaos.

own destruction. We are the faithful ones, whose souls will be saved" (Hebrews 10:38-39).

Quoting the prophet Habakkuk, the author of the letter to the Hebrews challenges us not to give up trusting God in times of persecution or suffering. The preservation of life is the fruit of this trust in God. Precisely because we have access to the Lord through Jesus, we can ask Him for help not to lose heart in the waiting room.

It was discouraging for Habakkuk to hear that an arrogant, wicked, and self-sufficient people would touch God's chosen people. But it was as if the Almighty were saying to his prophet, "Habakkuk, trust me, for I know what I am doing."

When a father waits for his son to break free from the grip of drugs or a wife prays for her husband to treat her differently and answers are delayed, they need to keep their focus on God's words: "Live trusting in me." Therefore, the hope of one day getting out of the long stay in the waiting room is the fruit of the decision to continue in the firm and unwavering decision to trust God. When Habakkuk decided to go up to the watchtower, he was saying, "I will be alone with God to hear what he has to say to me." In other words, he was stating, "I'm going to stop asking and start praying." Yes, in the waiting room we discover the power of prayer, which became tangible in Habakkuk's life as he went up to the watchtower.

One morning in the waiting room my wife brought me deep encouragement from God. She had written in her prayer journal: "Bless me during this time with you, my mighty Father." Being alone with God is our daily blessing, which gives us the nourishment to survive together in waiting rooms. Over the years, we have discovered that greater than the answer to our prayers is the presence of the Lord. Our hearts are set on God because of who he is, and because of that we can worship and praise him.

During our prayer time in the waiting room, we realized how God takes us from despair to hope, how faith is developed and strengthened, and this allows us see that hope does not disappoint.

4

The World Outside the Waiting Room

Violence, evil, and corruption

João Carlos was a brilliant student at a famous science and technology school in his home state. Since childhood, he had always been fascinated by information technology and by his first years of college, he was already developing smartphone apps. Two years after graduating, in partnership with two classmates, he developed an app that caught the attention of several companies and an investor. It seemed that his dream would come true. The investor sponsored the project, guaranteed full financial support during the development of the app, and became familiar with it.

When the project was over, the investor dropped the idea. He took all the coordinates and the secrets of João Carlos's project to another group of developers. As a result, he and his friends lost the project, the funding, and almost three years of hard work in research and development. The three friends had grown up in the church, where they worked with a group of university students. Disappointed, they began to wonder why God had allowed this.

Habakkuk had similar feelings and thoughts. In chapter 2 of his book, we find him waiting for God to answer his questions. Although the Lord reaffirms that he will use the

Babylonians to punish the kingdom of Judah, the description of the wickedness of those people gives the prophet hope.

Like João Carlos, who experienced the investor stealing his project and making a lot of money from it, we will all face situations that are as painful as facing persecution from "Babylonians." João Carlos's ex-investor became a kind of Babylonian for him. How could he handle the wickedness of the heart of the one who had deceived him?

In order answer this, we must first understand that all evil is due to the presence of sin in the human heart. It would be simple to attribute responsibility for the wickedness of the world to God, since it is a fact that he is sovereign and controls all things. But we cannot forget that man bears responsibility for his actions. Yet sinful acts do not hinder or change God's plans. On the contrary, he uses them without relieving us of our responsibility. The Creator did not create evil. It is the consequence of sinful humanity's disobedience.

Our stay in the waiting room may stem from the evil present in the world or from its direct action in our lives. The Babylonians, João Carlos's former investor, and the driver who caused the accident involving Joubert may have all made different mistakes with different consequences, but they all practiced evil simply because they are sinners (Romans 3:23).

Arrogance and idolatry

God used the Babylonians despite their sinful lifestyle. It is interesting to note that God reveals to Habakkuk that *arrogance and idolatry* are the reason for their wickedness and, ultimately, for everyone's wickedness.

Arrogant people harbor emptiness and seek to fill it with anything that will satisfy them, inflate their egos, and expand their inner selves. Sadly, this process generates slavery, downfall, and death. These selfish actions that attempt to fill this void are characterized by self-sufficiency, excessive vanity, a quest for power, control, wealth, dominance, authority, success and prominence, and a desire for fame and superiority. We see this in religious church leaders who are focused on numbers, the power of their influence, invitations to theological conferences, the recognition of famous people in Christian circles, and the like.

The appetites of proud people are never satisfied. Their fatal dilemma is that they are self-centered and try to satisfy themselves from the wrong sources. Their search for inner satisfaction is insatiable and this drives them to hunt for prey that they can devour and dominate. This is how the Babylonians acted: "Wealth is treacherous, and the arrogant are never at rest. They open their mouths as wide as the grave, and like death, they are never satisfied. In their greed they have gathered up many nations and swallowed many peoples" (Habakkuk 2:5).

These words, which refer primarily to the Babylonians, bear uncanny resemblance to the actions of modern day rulers or political leaders who give and receive bribes, cut down forests for economic interests, and have unbridled sex lives. All of these are the actions of a proud humanity trying everything to fill the emptiness of their souls. The hunger to satisfy an arrogant person's ego is so immense that they consider themselves self-sufficient, putting themselves in God's place and feeling no need for accountability. The law of the proud becomes their own measure; God's principles and values are forgotten and rejected as abominations.

This insatiable hunger for economic power led João Carlos's former investor to disregard his word and forget God's limits, setting his own criteria. In doing so, he harmed João Carlos and sent him to the waiting room. The actions of the Babylonians and the former investor differ in practice, but are the same in essence: pride, arrogance, haughtiness.

Pride not only leads us away from God, it also makes us forget that Jesus is what really fulfills us. We stop seeking God's best for us. Proverbs 6:16-19 shows us that arrogance tops the list of things that God hates:

> There are six things the Lord hates—
> no, seven things he detests:
> haughty eyes,
> a lying tongue,
> hands that kill the innocent,
> a heart that plots evil,
> feet that race to do wrong,
> a false witness who pours out lies,
> a person who sows discord in a family.

But arrogance was not the only problem with the Babylonians' perverse lifestyle. Along with their prideful spirit was idolatry:

> What good is an idol carved by man,
> or a cast image that deceives you?
> How foolish to trust in your own creation—
> a god that can't even talk!
> What sorrow awaits you who say to wooden idols,
> "Wake up and save us!"
> To speechless stone images you say,
> "Rise up and teach us!"
> Can an idol tell you what to do?

> They may be overlaid with gold and silver,
> but they are lifeless inside.
> But the LORD is in his holy Temple.
> Let all the earth be silent before him.

Habakkuk 2:18-20

The Babylonians worshipped images carved out of metal by human hands. God says that these idols are worthless and it is foolish to trust them. The Babylonians uselessly tried to talk to them. Their monetary value did not change the impossibility and inability to guide the people. While we may be tempted to consider these people unintelligent, don't we ourselves in the middle of the 21st century erect idols or proclaim gods?

A god is a source from which we seek to draw or receive satisfaction, direction, provision, protection, and life purpose. When we find them, our hearts are filled and we experience satisfaction, however illusory or fleeting. The Babylonians built gods of silver and gold, but they didn't find satisfaction, direction, provision, protection, or purpose in those statues. So they adopted a lifestyle full of violence, extortion, and corruption. Why? Because the satisfaction they desired can only be found in God, through Christ. Their pursuit was like chasing the wind, which did not bring lasting fulfillment or true accomplishment.

Today, we may not bow down to idols built by human hands, but we do use our time that should be dedicated to our children, spouse, or God to do whatever is necessary to get a promotion, earn more money, or gain more recognition and power. Conversely, our families can become the greatest idol we hold in our hearts, as the hunger for a happy family breeds pride and idolatry. If we believe that the source of our happiness is our spouse and children instead of God, we are idolizing them. There is nothing wrong with having a happy family or wanting to quickly climb a few steps in the corporate world. The problem is when we turn these things into "gods." Among Christians, sometimes the idol is not the perfect family, but the perfect morality. We want to be perfect believers, as if we were justified not by faith but by our behavior. If we are morally irreproachable, we believe that we are justified and end up discriminating against those who fail.

The Babylonians were also known to continually get drunk on "strong drinks" to create an atmosphere for lustful practices (Habakkuk 2:15, BBE). Even sex can become a god when we overlook the fact that it is a gift to be enjoyed in marriage or when we make it our greatest source of satisfaction. Like the Babylonians, when we turn a lie into a truth, we hold people hostage. We give "strong drink" to others so we can use them. And it is not just alcohol. We use manipulation, flattery, and seduction with sweet and deceptive words. The problem is that some idols, such as sex, provide immediate pleasure, but they generate emptiness afterwards.

Today, many other things have become idols: control, money, beauty, and individuality. None of this is bad in itself. It is not wrong to want to maintain a healthy body, to buy new houses or cars, to dream of a normal, well-adjusted family, to have a budget under control, and things of that sort. The problem arises when these things become more important than God in our lives.

An idol of the heart is anything we imagine we can't live without. In his book *Counterfeit Gods*, Tim Keller writes that an idol of the heart "has such a controlling position in your heart that you can spend most of your passion and energy, your emotional and financial resources, on it without a second thought."[1]

Today's problems are no different from those that the Babylonians personified. The Babylonians, João Carlos's former investor, and we ourselves are proud and idolatrous. There is no denying it. But when we act arrogantly or make use of idols while in a waiting room, the situation will worsen and certainly prevent us from coming out of it in a healthy way.

The good news is that God has the solution to human arrogance and idolatry.

God deals with arrogance and idolatry

Godless people wreak havoc because of sin, which directly assails the values of the Lord. Thus, it is normal for God to discipline them in His own time and way. It was the same with the Babylonians. God refers several times to the their actions and the discipline that would come upon them as a result of their sins. They stole, coveted, killed, committed adultery, acted arrogantly, and worshipped idols (Habakkuk 2:6, 9, 12, 15, 19). The Babylonians acted as if they were self-sufficient and independent from God, but the Lord was not indifferent to what was happening. It was evident that not only Israel would be punished but the Babylonians also, for no one who rebels against God goes unpunished.

Yet the Lord does not punish the wicked ones who harm us solely because of what they have done against us, but because their actions are completely contrary to his holiness and justice.

It is therefore not our role, but God's, to act as avenger. God's actions against the Babylonians also serve as a lesson for us. We should reflect on whether we are also susceptible to God's discipline because of pride and idolatry. We must not forget that even though nothing can separate us from his love, God also disciplines those he loves.

The fact is that the righteous often suffer while the wicked and perverse prosper. This was partly the reason for Habakkuk's distress, and often becomes ours as well. In Psalms 73:11-14, Asaph expresses these same feelings:

> "What does God know?" they ask.
> "Does the Most High even know what's happening?"
> Look at these wicked people—
> enjoying a life of ease while their riches multiply.
> Did I keep my heart pure for nothing?
> Did I keep myself innocent for no reason?
> I get nothing but trouble all day long;
> every morning brings me pain.

These could well be João Carlos's words. He had tried to live righteously all his life, but then saw the man who defrauded him quietly escape the situation and become richer than before. Upon entering God's sanctuary, the Asaph redirects his thinking: "Then I went into your sanctuary, O God, and I finally understood the destiny of the wicked" (Psalm 73:17).

> We must not forget that even though nothing can separate us from his love, God also disciplines those he loves.

Habakkuk was about to experience the same situation as the psalmist. We too can face this same sense of abandonment by God and as a result become skeptical and distrustful when hearing Scripture. We can also be led to give up on trusting

God. Fortunately, Habakkuk and Asaph made the right decision. Asaph entered the sanctuary and Habakkuk went up to the watchtower. When we go through crises or frightening scenarios, the most encouraging thing is not to focus on the extent of the problem but, like the prophet, to listen and learn more of the Lord:

> Has not the Lord Almighty determined
>> that the people's labor is only fuel for the fire,
>> that the nations exhaust themselves for nothing?
> For the earth will be filled with the knowledge
>>> of the glory of the Lord
>> as the waters cover the sea.

Habakkuk 2:13-14 (NIV)

While God sees the Babylonians' corruption and violence, he also makes it clear that he will act in an unprecedented way to overthrow them and make himself known throughout the earth. The world was experiencing the Babylonians' power, violence, and immorality, but in an even deeper and more extensive way, it would come to know the power of God. While the knowledge of the Babylonians' power brought destruction, the knowledge of God brought freedom and a relationship with God Himself.

It is important to note the expression "knowledge of the glory of the Lord." The word "knowledge" in this context means much more than just an awareness of something. In the Old Testament, the concept of the knowledge of God includes the idea of relationship and powerful presence.[2] To know God means to have a personal relationship with him, and to have experienced his presence and his attributes, such as love, peace, and joy. To know God means to have intimacy with him (Exodus 33:17).

So when the Lord tells Habakkuk that the earth would be filled with the knowledge of God, he meant that despite the world's corruption, it would have the opportunity to see and experience the divine presence. God had in mind not only the impact that the fall of the Babylonians would cause but also what would happen when future generations came to know him through the Messiah. Thus, in Christ, the whole earth would be filled with the knowledge and the presence of God, and people would have a relationship with Him.

> To know God means to have a personal relationship with him, to have experienced his presence and his attributes, such as love, peace and joy.

It is a source of great hope to know that God is not blind to the actions of the wicked, the perverse, and the proud and that he has his eyes open to bless the chosen ones with his presence. Knowing that God will act and reveal Himself should reassure our hearts when we end up in the waiting room due to the mistakes of others and the evil that is active in the world.

Instead of focusing on the loneliness of his waiting room, João Carlos's challenge was to focus on a God whose holy character does not let sin go unpunished. Like Habakkuk, João Carlos was getting to know an all-powerful God, but also one who desires a personal relationship with those who follow him and suffer in the waiting room. Habakkuk saw a God who acts on behalf of his own and at the same time aims to punish the wicked.

By realizing that God would punish the Babylonians, Habakkuk is able to reconcile the purpose of a holy God. It is as if God is telling the prophet: "Calm down, Habakkuk, the story does not end with the Babylonians. They are wicked, but they are in my hands." So he continues: "But the LORD is in his holy Temple. Let all the earth be silent before him" (Habbakkuk 2:20). Habakkuk accepts God's sovereignty, and it silences him. His inquisitive, anxious, and protesting spirit in the beginning of his book gives way to an attitude of humility and submission to God. The time in the watchtower brought healing to the prophet's weary soul. God's holiness was defended and recognized. In contrast to the Babylonian gods, who were always silent and powerless, Habakkuk is silent before the all-powerful, but also personal and loving sovereign God.

To be silent before God is not to be silent because the Lord does not hear us. Silence is that sense of security that God's presence offers in times of distress, questioning, and uncertainty. Being in his holy temple does not mean that the Most High is in a room made of bricks and mortar, but that he is everywhere, with us in the chaos or in the celebration. So we can be quiet, silent, secure.

The Babylonians' divine punishment took place in 539 BC. Their pride and idolatry collapsed under the new power of the Medo-Persians. During a banquet in which the king of Babylon dishonored God and used the utensils of the temple in the midst of drunkenness and orgies, the Lord announced the defeat—that very night—of the Babylonian kingdom to the conqueror Darius (Daniel 5:1-31).

Like Habakkuk, the psalmist Asaph comes to his senses and runs to God: "Then I went into your sanctuary, O God, and I finally understood the destiny of the wicked. Truly, you put them on a slippery path and send them sliding over the cliff to destruction. In an instant they are destroyed, completely swept away by terrors" (Psalm 73:17-19). Eventually, those who—as the Babylonians—live arrogantly and independently of God, will also fall.

Instead of dwelling on his loss and devising a means for revenge, João Carlos was learning that the same God who allowed the deception was also the God who would take care of him and deal with the offender's injustice.

How do we deal with the culture of pride and idolatry that influences us?

God, Habakkuk, and us

Before looking at the Babylonians' horrendous sin with an air of moral superiority, we must remember that we are as sinful as they are and are therefore subject to the same discipline. God, however, always has a path to restoration if we repent of our arrogance and idolatry. From our waiting room, we must first ask God: "Search me, O God, and know my heart; test me and know my anxious thoughts. Point out anything in me that offends you, and lead me along the path of everlasting life" (Psalm 139:23-24). We cannot assume that we are not proud or that we do not have other gods. Instead, we should ask ourselves some brave questions, such as: "What do I truly think I cannot afford to lose in life?"; "What disappoints me the most?"; "Do I often complain to my spouse about our sex life?"; "Do I fight too much when people are disrespectful to me?"; "Does the fear of running out of money prevent me from contributing regularly to the church?" These are questions that help us check whether we have gods inside us, whether they be ego, sex, or money. Remember that your extended time in one of life's waiting rooms may be the context in which God is warning you, "Hey, you're on the Babylonian path. Repent and come back."

Some time ago, I discovered a major "god" in my life. Whenever I preached a sermon and nobody praised it, I felt a tremendous void. I discovered that often my preaching wasn't done to serve God but to try to build my image as a preacher. This was painful to accept, but my wife lovingly confronted me about it, and since then the Lord has been working in my heart. I needed to confess my sin, and every time this god tries to resurface, I run to the Father to confess this attempt to "fill myself" in the wrong way.

False gods try to inflate our ego and need to be identified, confronted, confessed, and abandoned. The point is that we cannot deal with our gods or forsake them without looking to Jesus and seeking his intervention in our lives. He is the example, for though he is God, he emptied himself. When we acknowledge our sins and decide to believe in Christ as our Savior and Lord, our ego has a chance to deflate, and the void can be filled with divine love. We abandon idols when, after believing in Jesus, we start to value and seek what God approves.

The Babylonians' idolatry directed them towards power, control, fame, sex, and money. João Carlos created a god around the idea that if the project for the app had not been stolen, he and his friends would be rich and famous. But when Jesus occupies our hearts, our pursuit is redirected so that we become forgiving, generous, loving, and free from an obsession for power and control. We gradually and daily surrender control to God.

The Bible is very clear when it says: "Since you have been raised to new life with Christ, set your sights on the realities of heaven, where Christ sits in the place of honor at God's right hand" (Colossians 3:1). Whenever the idols of the heart and the swelling of the ego resurface, we need to refocus, reflect, and seek that which is related to God and His will for us.

It was a process for João Carlos to accept the app's success and even to watch other people benefiting from his work without receiving the rewards of his effort. His inner issue was to be able to look at the situation from the sovereign God's perspective instead of looking at it with "Babylonian" eyes.

We cannot let resentment against "Babylonians" dominate us. God will ultimately take care of them. As Paul wrote in Romans 12:19-21:

> Dear friends, never take revenge. Leave that to the righteous anger of God. For the Scriptures say, "I will take revenge; I will pay them back," says the Lord. Instead, "If your enemies are hungry, feed them. If they are thirsty, give them something to drink. In doing this, you will heap burning coals of shame on their heads." Don't let evil conquer you, but conquer evil by doing good.

The longer I postpone the forgiveness I need to extend to the Babylonian who has wronged me, the more I become his slave and bow down to him, wanting to take revenge. This is idolatry and pride. Idolatry because sometimes I think that the day I take revenge, I will feel better, which generates guilt, and without Jesus I will have no victory over guilt. Pride because, as I dwell on the "Babylonian's" harmful actions, my ego and my desire to take the place of God are inflated.

So I need to run to Jesus. And you do, too.

5

Rejoicing in God in the Waiting Room

It is possible to be happy when the focus is not on the problems

As soon as I arrived at the Morumbi Baptist Church, the congregation that I now pastor, my wife and I were warmly welcomed by Jeremias and Grace, a couple who inspired us greatly and with whom we became friends. They had been in the city for a few years, had a beautiful family, and were successful in their business endeavors.

Things were going very well until the day they discovered that their business partner was cheating them; they suddenly lost everything but the house they lived in. In the midst of the financial crisis, one of the sons got his girlfriend pregnant. Shortly afterwards, creditors started trying to collect debts they did not even know existed, the result of the former partner's unlawful actions. Since the swindler had transferred his assets to a third party, Jeremias and Grace found themselves obliged to honor the debts of the bankrupt company.

Then Jeremias fell seriously ill, and the purchase of expensive medicines further deepened their financial crisis. As the debts increased, their lawyer asked them to sign a document falsely stating that they were living on the poverty line, so that they could better negotiate what they owed. The couple resisted because, although they were almost bankrupt, the meager pension they received prevented them from going hungry. Not wanting to lie, they refused.

One day, the couple came to talk to me. They weren't asking for help, or for me to pray for them. They had just come to hug me on my birthday. During our meeting, they didn't even touch on the subject of their pain, debts, and losses, nor the issue of Jeremias' illness. As a pastor, I am very used to hearing stories of suffering and despair, but this case was different. Jeremias and Grace came to me not to share their burden, but to encourage me because they knew my wife and I were going through difficult times with our children. After they prayed for us, I asked them how they managed to be so calm despite the storm they were going through. And their answer has a lot to do with Habakkuk's circumstances.

In chapter 3, we see a very different man from the one presented in chapter 1. The prophet is no longer a restless, dissatisfied, or questioning person. The waiting room had become a fortress and a place of hope and satisfaction, even though he had not yet received the answers he expected. Habakkuk had never possessed the wealth that Jeremias and Grace once enjoyed, but he was discovering something more precious and fulfilling.

How did Habakkuk manage to stay in the waiting room without complaining about life or God's delay in getting him out? How do people like Jeremias and Grace manage to live serenely, without being overwhelmed by seemingly unmet needs?

While we are in the waiting room, we can nurture a bitter or a grateful heart. If we focus on the fact that God could have prevented what brought us to the waiting room, we plant seeds of bitterness. But if, in the midst of silence and solitude, we decide to focus on what God wants to produce in us, we reduce anxiety and grow in confidence. Long hours in the waiting room brings physical and emotional fatigue, but in this context we can focus on what Jesus said: "Come to me, all of you who are weary and carry heavy burdens, and I will give you rest" (Matthew 11:28).

When we are immersed in the hustle and bustle of our daily schedules, we hardly value Jesus's words, because in a way we feel that we are in control of things. But in the helplessness of life's waiting rooms, we learn how to enjoy the emotional rest God wants to give us. I believe that is why Habakkuk says: "I trembled inside when I heard this; my lips quivered with fear. My legs gave way beneath me, and I shook in terror. I will wait quietly for the coming day when disaster will strike the people who invade us" (Habakkuk 3:16).

It is remarkable to compare these words of Habakkuk in chapter 3 with what the prophet had said shortly before in chapter 1: "How long, O Lord, must I call for help? But you do not listen! 'Violence is everywhere!' I cry, but you do not come to save" (v. 2). What changed in God's story with Habakkuk? Nothing. God's plans to send the Babylonians to punish Israel remained intact. In truth, it was Habakkuk who had changed.

Perhaps Habakkuk had not fully understood how God works, but his trust in the Lord was visibly strengthened. His prolonged time in the watchtower had not hardened his heart. As he waited for God's response to his complaints (2:1), the prophet discovered that anxiety would not shorten his time of waiting; instead, this period brought relief to his soul. As he spoke to God, he began to see the situation from God's perspective. The reassured soul—full of hope and focused on

God's grace—is capable of not despairing in the face of the slow ticking of the waiting room clock.

When I asked Jeremias and Grace how they managed to remain so calm in the midst of their storm, I silently wondered how I would respond in the midst of a storm. This led me to look at that stage of Habakkuk's life as a possible response for me and for you. We all go through moments when our lips quiver, our legs falter, and our bodies tremble with terror. It is very difficult to see what we have long dreamed of achieving suddenly disappear. It might be the house that we financed for more than 15 years that catches fire right after it's been paid off, and whose insurance we didn't renew because we just forgot. It is the dream marriage that ends after only two months because the spouse dies due to medical error. But Habakkuk's trembling goes from being fixated on the Babylonians to being focused on the majesty of God.

> What changed in God's story with Habakkuk? Nothing. God's plans to send the Babylonians to punish Israel remain intact. In truth, it was Habakkuk who had changed.

Habakkuk was discovering a powerful and personal God like he had never known before. At this point in the account, his trembling is no longer about fear but about the privilege of witnessing and experiencing God's power which can provide peace and security even in the face of the imminent danger of the Babylonians. Having an intimate experience with God in a waiting room filled with pain, coldness, anxiety, stagnation, and despair transforms our lives and makes us tremble. But it is a trembling associated with trust. As Larry Crabb wrote: "Tremble when God's direction doesn't make sense, but without ceasing to trust the God who allows nothing to hinder his purposes."[1]

While we are in the waiting room, we do not know how everything will turn out; because we have no control over events, and this can upset and unsettle us. Nevertheless, God's presence produces a consistent sense of security when we remember who he is and the faithfulness of his love. When we focus on the Almighty, confidence in his presence and power becomes stronger than the fear generated by circumstances. And that is what I began to see in Jeremias and Grace. Though they were living in the midst of a seemingly endless storm, their focus was on the infinite power of God, who— they trusted— would in due time turn the storm into a shower of blessings.

My wife and I trembled when the neonatologist told us that our son would not walk, talk, or hear, and that the likelihood of a healthy, normal life was remote. For a while, the family dream seemed to have turned into a nightmare. But when we shift our focus, changes happen. Not necessarily in the circumstances, but in us, and these transformations are led by God.

Trading anxiety for peace and rest

Anxiety robs us of peace. Fear reflects insecurity. If we don't have an anchor to hold us steady in the midst of a process of loss, we feel desperate, insecure, and fearful. As Maurício Zágari has written: "fear generates anxiety and anxiety generates fear. They often merge and blend with each other, becoming a single, terrifying monster".[2]

This is how it was for the disciples who aboard the boat with Jesus during that powerful storm on the Sea of Galilee:

> As evening came, Jesus said to his disciples, "Let's cross to the other side of the lake." So they took Jesus in the boat and started out, leaving the crowds behind (although other boats followed). But soon a fierce storm came up. High waves were breaking into the boat, and it began to fill with water.
>
> Jesus was sleeping at the back of the boat with his head on a cushion. The disciples woke him up, shouting, "Teacher, don't you care that we're going to drown?"
>
> When Jesus woke up, he rebuked the wind and said to the waves, "Silence! Be still!" Suddenly the wind stopped, and there was a great calm. Then he asked them, "Why are you afraid? Do you still have no faith?"
>
> The disciples were absolutely terrified. "Who is this man?" they asked each other. "Even the wind and waves obey him!"
>
> Mark 4:35-41

It is not difficult to imagine the scene. Although as fishermen many of those men were experienced in navigating that region, they had never faced a problem of that magnitude before. Their previous experiences hadn't provided them with the serenity needed to deal with such overwhelming waves. There are similarities between this situation and that of Habakkuk. It was strange for the anxious and frightened disciples to see Jesus sleeping as if nothing were happening. How could he be free from anxiety and fear?

Christ's tranquility was the result of his certainty about who he was and in whom he trusted. Remember that although he was God, he was also man, and in his humanity he was subject to facing all the we face. The same trust that Jesus had in the

Father is the kind the Father wants us to have. That's why the storms and waiting rooms of life are so valuable. Jesus commanded the wind that was causing the storm and those huge waves to just "Be still!" The men had no power over the wind, but Jesus did. That's why he could sleep peacefully.

Initially, Habakkuk went through a period of anxiety and turmoil, but he was learning to hear God say, "Be still!" And even though the storm was not yet over, the prophet's heart was stilled. When he said that he would wait "quietly" for the day when disaster would come upon the invaders (3:16), he clearly had abundant peace at that moment. From trembling, fear, insecurity, and anxiety, he moved on to peace of mind. The prophet had discovered that security is not in the absence of conflict, but in the powerful presence of God.

> The prophet had discovered that security is not in the absence of conflict, but in the powerful presence of God.

The Hebrew verb used by Habakkuk and translated as "I will wait"[3] has the sense of resting after work. It was as if he were saying, "I will rest after my struggles to understand what is happening." No one rests if they are not at peace. Without rest, anxiety causes sleepless nights. The prophet's rest was also a sign of satisfaction. He was now satisfied with what God had told him in the watchtower. Getting what we hope for isn't what ultimately satisfies our souls because that too will pass away, deteriorate, and be lost. This type of satisfaction and relief is temporary. The greatest and most permanent satisfaction comes from communion with God, in spite of all circumstances. This satisfaction will remain.

Jeremias and Grace told me that they were holding up strong because whenever fear overwhelmed them, they talked to God about their anxiety. They learned to give thanks for what they had in the past, secure in the knowledge that God had something even better for them. And, along with gratitude, they continued to pray for the unknown future, believing that the God of the past would remain with them. This gave them the assurance they needed. Loss was no longer so significant to them when compared to what they were experiencing at that stage of life.

The book of Habakkuk begins with a prayer, at a time when the prophet was disappointed, anxious, and almost desperate. It was a prayer of lament, of a deep expression of fear, and of nonconformity with the situation. The prophet also begins chapter three by praying, during his inner transformation. Certainly, Habakkuk's time in the watchtower was a period of prayer and answers.

In the face of pressure, prayer is almost the last resort. But it should be the first. When we pray, we put God back in the spotlight instead of the problems. Habakkuk chapter three is a lesson in how to pray during difficult times, when God seems distant or slow to answer our outcry. It brings words of worship and deep trust in God, highlighting his great deeds of the past.

Jeremias and Grace shared with me that God had blessed them with their first business by guiding them to quit their jobs and start their own company. It was also God who had given them their first clients, and multiplied them more and more. And in that difficult phase when they still didn't understand the chaos in which they found themselves, the couple remembered what God had done in the past, renewing their certainty that prayer was the answer.

When we are in situations of danger, fear, or anxiety, our prayer usually focuses on the relief we desire: "Lord, take us out of this cold waiting room!" It would be so meaningful to pray, "Lord, no matter how long I'm in this room, I pray that you will be glorified." It was by focusing on what he had heard about God in the past that Habakkuk prayed with this purpose. He was certain that just as God had acted in the past, he could act again in the present. This is the fruit of spiritual maturity, something that comes not from emotion but from knowing the truth about the Lord.

Habakkuk recalls God's deeds that had generated in him an thrill of trembling and reverence. This part of the prayer has a remarkable application to our lives. Remembering God's actions and his attributes nourishes our faith, strengthens our transformative journey, and leads us to achieve satisfaction. This satisfaction in God becomes more remarkable than the solution to the problem.

In a poetic tone, Habakkuk recalls how God appeared to his people in the past: "His brilliant splendor fills the heavens, and the earth is filled with his praise. His coming is as brilliant as the sunrise. Rays of light flash from his hands, where his awesome power is hidden" (Habakkuk 3:3-4). God had appeared in brilliant splendor to his people in the past, on the journey from Egypt to the promised land. And filled with the the Holy Spirit, we have the brilliance of God's presence within us today, enabling us to experience divine love in the midst of fear, and providing security.

Habakkuk describes God's actions in breaking the proud Pharaoh's heart in the time of Moses: "Pestilence marches before him; plague follows close behind. When he stops, the earth shakes. When he looks, the nations tremble. He shatters the everlasting mountains and levels the eternal hills. He is the Eternal One!" (Habakkuk 3:5-6). The significance of the plagues in Egypt points to God's power over everything that rises up against him. And this power was known to the people of antiquity.[4] The plagues and pestilences against Egypt were a message from God to the Egyptians and Israelites: the gods of Egypt had no power at all.

We too have our gods and there comes a time when God wishes to destroy them. It is only when we run to the Lord, giving up the control of these gods over us, that he delivers us from them. Our gods may give us some passing pleasure, but only God's ways are eternal. So when he allows certain plagues to come upon us, it is because he wants to deliver us from false gods. The plagues may be sickness, financial failure, loss of relationships, or anything else that takes the place of the Lord in our lives.

Two historical facts come to the prophet's mind in this part of the prayer:

> The mountains watched and trembled.
> Onward swept the raging waters.
> The mighty deep cried out,
> lifting its hands in submission.
> The sun and moon stood still in the sky
> as your brilliant arrows flew
> and your glittering spear flashed.
> You marched across the land in anger
> and trampled the nations in your fury.
> You went out to rescue your chosen people,
> to save your anointed ones.
> You crushed the heads of the wicked
> and stripped their bones from head to toe.

Habakkuk 3:10-13

Habakkuk had not seen the sun or the moon stand still, as understood from the account in Joshua 10:12-15, but he had heard about and believed God's deeds to help his people that day. Despite the large contingent of enemy armies that fought against Joshua, God's presence with his people was enough to give them victory. How exactly that phenomenon came about was not Habakkuk's main concern; rather, it was to understand that divine intervention had come in response to Joshua's prayer. Just as God had performed a cosmic miracle to protect his people from their enemies, he would continue to preserve the Israelites. Thus, Joshua's prayer resonates with Habakkuk's. The God of cosmic miracles is the God of miracles in health, financial life, business failure, broken relationships, drug, or sex addiction. Nothing stands in the way of his plans.

"With his own weapons, you destroyed the chief of those who rushed out like a whirlwind, thinking Israel would be easy prey. You trampled the sea with your horses, and the mighty waters piled high" (3:14-15). This was the experience of God's people when facing the pharaoh's persecution and the impassability of the Red Sea. If they stopped, they would be captured, and if they continued, they would be overtaken. What now? Habakkuk recalls that God parted the sea and destroyed the force that sought to capture his people. In Exodus 14:14, Moses told the people: "The LORD himself will fight for you. Just stay calm."

When we are in the waiting room for a seemingly unsolvable problem, remembering what God has done with his chosen ones renews our confidence in the truth that he will not leave us facing an impassable sea. He will either open the sea or let us enter the water without drowning. When the time is right, he will open the door out of the waiting room so that we may move on to a new moment in life, characterized by rest in him.

> When the time is right,
> he will open the door
> out of the waiting room
> so that we may move on
> to a new moment in life,
> characterized by rest in him.

In Habakkuk's mind, the memory of these deeds generates the certainty that God delivers his people and strengthens their hearts. Even in the difficult, tenuous, and time-consuming waiting room, the prophet is being cared for by God and demonstrates his passion for his people. He knew that despite the Babylonians' power, the same God who had delivered and protected the nation against the Egyptians would somehow preserve his chosen ones. It is important to note that preserving did not mean that the Lord would avoid bloodshed, but that he would not fail to fulfill his plans for the nation.

It is by understanding this that Habakkuk says: "I will wait quietly for the coming day when disaster will strike the people who invade us" (Habakkuk 3:16). He is at peace now. The God who stopped the sun and the moon and who opened the Red Sea is giving him the answer that he wanted to know when he withdrew to the watchtower. Habakkuk was not discovering a God who merely solves problems, but the God who satisfies. The prophet is not benefiting from a utilitarian God who lives to serve him, but is experiencing a relationship with the God who satisfies his inner self, even though he knew the Babylonians would invade Israel.

We need to keep in mind that remembering God's deeds in the past is related to our time walking with him. Passing through the Red Sea, crossing the Jordan River "on dry feet" and seeing the sun and moon stand still were not experiences that happened overnight. Experiences with God that produce solid and permanent spiritual growth are experienced over years.

These memories reaffirmed the prophet's belief that the Lord loved him. It is important to remember that the record of these deeds can only be found in the Bible, so if we do not invest in daily or regular time in reading God's Word and applying it to our lives, how can we face the long hours, or days, in waiting rooms? The changes in Habakkuk's heart were wrought through prayer and by remembering what God had done in the past, as it was recorded in Scripture. Surely the prophet's time in the watchtower included time alone with the Father. Shouldn't we follow the same path?

It is common to see people praise God when their problems are solved. After being healed of an illness, we offer a thanksgiving service as an expression of our gratitude. But I have never seen anyone offer a thanksgiving service to God while still in the midst of illness, before the problem has been resolved.

It is important to note that Habakkuk shows his satisfaction and gratitude not after his problem is solved, but while he is still in the waiting room, in the eye of the hurricane. God did not tell him that he had changed his plans. Adversity was sure to come, but even so the prophet shows satisfaction, because his focus turns from the circumstances to God.

There is an extraordinary moment in chapter 3, between verses 16 and 18:

I hear, and I tremble within;
my lips quiver at the sound.
Rottenness enters into my bones,

and my steps tremble beneath me.
I wait quietly for the day of calamity
to come upon the people who attack us.

Though the fig tree does not blossom
and no fruit is on the vines;
though the produce of the olive fails
and the fields yield no food;
though the flock is cut off from the fold
and there is no herd in the stalls,
yet I will rejoice in the Lord;
I will exult in the God of my salvation.

Habakkuk 3:16-18, NRSVUE

Notice the contrast between the state of trembling, fear, and dread in verse 16 and the state of hope, peace, and rest in verses 17 and 18. This contrast shows how Habakkuk learned to be content and to rest in God in the midst of the waiting room trials. He didn't wait until the problem was solved before exalting God, who was the source of his joy.

If we were facing the same moral, economic, and social bankruptcy, how would we react? It is important to note Habakkuk's reaction. His losses were not leading him to despair, but to a deeper relationship with God. Only when we go deeper in our relationship with the Father are we able to say that we will continue to trust God and rejoice in him even if we lose everything. In the silence of the waiting room and despite his anguish, the prophet glorifies God and experiences rest, peace, and great intimacy with the Lord.

Our challenge in the waiting room is to discover that God is good, even when we are lonely, when the dependent drug-addicted child relapses into addiction, when we face divorce, marital infidelity, or abandonment. In short, it means that we can find peace and rest amidst the greatest problems.

To understand what Habakkuk meant by the expression "yet I will rejoice in the Lord; I will exult in the God of my salvation!," we need to focus on the nouns "joy" and "exultation." Both communicate what is in the prophet's heart, each with its own characteristics. The word "joy" refers to an experience of triumph, that inner or emotional experience that generates singing and gratitude. It is the natural response we offer or feel in the face of God's faithfulness. On the other hand, "exultation," while also carrying the sense of joy and rejoicing, differs in denoting a greater intensity. Of course, Habakkuk is not laughing, but the anxiety he had previously felt has been alleviated. So he is able to both wait in silence for the day when adversity would strike his invaders and to rejoice and exult in the Lord.

It is also important to note that in the context of Habakkuk's experience, the idea of salvation was not exactly our concept of forgiveness of sins and reconciliation with God through Jesus. It had to do with imminent danger. The Babylonians rejoiced in devastating and ending their captives' lives. However, even though the nation of Israel could have been an easy prey for the Babylonians, God was the prophet's security. The Lord had promised to discipline the nation because of sin, but also to preserve and restore it after their suffering. The prophet's rest was not based on a triumphalist feeling and rejection of the reality of danger, but on the inner certainty that God was faithful and would save him from chaos and abandonment, even if he did not know how he would be personally affected.

In summary, the prophet prayed, expressing his frustrations or exalting God. He remembered the deeds of the Lord and enjoyed his presence, which gave him peace and rest in the midst of chaos. And all of this finally translated into trust. But we still need to answer a crucial question. What was behind this process that led him from despair to hope?

Being a prophet, naturally Habakkuk knew the Old Testament—the divinely inspired and revealed Scriptures up to that time—and therefore he knew the Law well. So we can also assume that what led to the experience of prayer, remembrance, and trust and that fed Habakkuk's life of faith were the Law and some of the prophets' writings.

> The prophet's rest was not based on a triumphalist feeling and rejection of the reality of danger, but on the inner certainty that God was faithful and would save him from chaos and abandonment, even if he did not know how he would be personally affected.

Thinking about our own lives and our waiting rooms, we see a parallel that needs to be observed. If the Law and the prophets shaped Habakkuk's way of thinking, believing, and acting, shouldn't the same be true for us? How can we reflect at length in the waiting room if our minds are only occupied with anxiety? If we only have a vague idea of God, how will our soul be fed? After all, a fed soul is one that lives on the Word, and when we feed it, the mind discovers that God is the treasure and that our hearts must be focused on him. It is the discipline of reading the Scriptures and meditating on them that builds confidence in us and gives us the peace and rest we so yearn for.

In conversations with Jeremias and Grace, I discovered that Grace had the habit of memorizing verses: "What I have stored in my mind about God is what nourishes and sustains me in times of trial and when I face the temptation to give up," she told me. So, my question to you is: "What do you usually think about when you are in the waiting room? Do you focus on God's delay in responding? Do you focus on anxiety? Fear? Or do you remember what God's Word tells you?

The Word is the revelation of the Eternal. The more we embrace it as a shaper of our thoughts, the more strength we find to face the waiting rooms without faltering. Our greatest example is Jesus. He spent three years in a waiting room, between baptism and resurrection. How did Jesus endure such pressure? When tempted in the desert, he defeated

> Do you focus on God's delay in responding? Do you focus on anxiety? Fear? Or do you remember what God's Word tells you?

Satan simply by quoting the Scriptures. When questioned about divorce, he referred to Deuteronomy 24. In the hour of his death, amidst the anguish of being separated from the Father, he quoted Psalm 22. Our Savior could have responded to the pressures with his own words, for he was God, but he chose to use what was already written. And in the process of enduring the trial of Calvary, he knew that God would deliver him from the unbearable pain of the cross.

If Jesus turned to the Scriptures, where he found the Father's will, in order to endure the difficulties between baptism and resurrection, it becomes evident that the Word also needs to shape our lives before, during, and after our time in waiting rooms. We need to regularly invest time in reading the Scriptures, which will strengthen our love for God and our trust in Him.

When the government refused to provide the very expensive medication Jeremias needed to postpone the consequences of his illness, I did not see Grace question God. In fact, I heard her say to her husband, "God will provide, my love." I never saw either of them deny the pain they felt over their loss of possessions, position, and health, but they spoke of it without complaining.

In the few words that are recorded in Habakkuk 3:16-18, it seems like an eternity was lived during that short time. A man who was anxious and discontent with God's ways was transformed into a person who was joyful and exultant in God, despite the sorrows experienced and those yet to come. The ways of the Lord which at first seemed so meaningless in his eyes, were transformed into a path that pointed the way to future blessings.

In the waiting rooms of life, often the fig tree will not blossom, there will be no fruit on the vines, the olive harvest will come to nothing, the fields will be unproductive, herds will die in the fields, and the corrals will be empty. But this is not the end of the story. God will continue to act, despite everything.

Conclusion

Is it Possible to Leave the Waiting Room?

Habakkuk left the waiting room even though the problem had not been resolved. The Babylonians did attack the nation. What changed was the prophet's reaction. He rested and was at peace, despite the circumstances. Between the initial period of questioning and anxiety and the later moment of peace and joy, he discovered the God he had not previously known. The Lord took him from the insecurity of focusing on danger to the solace of focusing on the Lord. This is the same path that God wishes to walk with us. He always aims to lead us from despair to hope.

When Teodoro's doctor told Pedro and Dora that their baby would have consequences from the seizure, they feared and began to question again. But ultimately they discovered that the best way to face the disappointment of their son's illness was to trust in the sovereign God in whom they believed. Every day they would need to renew their trust in the Creator and Omnipotent God, understanding that if pure Love had allowed Theodore to become ill, it would also enable them to deal with the illness. Teodoro was slow to speak and walk, and he had learning difficulties in school, but Pedro and Dora saw God support the whole family in their son's gradual improvement. Every time Theodore has a seizure, they turn to the sovereign God who created their son and watches over his life. Believing in God's sovereignty gave the couple rest.

It is essential to know that God is sovereign. But even more significant is believing that it makes a difference in the lives of each one of us when we are in the waiting room. We can't change history, but we can choose to direct our eyes to the God who has the final word on all things. That is why Habakkuk could say: "The Sovereign LORD is my strength!" (Habakkuk 3:19). And because God was his strength, the prophet relied on him every day and in all circumstances. The Lord doesn't always eliminate our pains immediately, but He will certainly enable us and give us strength to deal with them.

It was very difficult and painful for Joubert's parents to see their athletic son—who had a wide and vibrant smile and had been full of life—leave the hospital in a wheelchair. Joubert was consoled, but his parents seemed to suffer a lot. It was a long time in the waiting room before they discovered that their sadness about the consequences of their son's accident and resentment toward the drunk driver could be exchanged for the daily strength that God gave them to deal with the pain in their souls. They would never have discovered the God who provides strength if they hadn't lived in a waiting room for a while. They discovered that true rest doesn't lie in a trouble-free life nor in the health of a child, but in trusting God.

> The Lord doesn't always eliminate our pains immediately, but He will certainly enable us and give us strength to deal with them.

Although Joubert did not leave for the mission field, he became a bivocational pastor. His administrative skills led him to direct an NGO with great social impact in the region where he lived. His master's in theology and postgraduate studies in human resources opened the door for him to work at a training center for future missionaries to the Muslim world. The sovereign and caring God turned a loss into a source of blessing for a large group of people. Despite living in a wheelchair, Joubert experiences the joy of living his life for God.

At the right time, our Father will open the door to the waiting room and tell us: "The wait is over."

Strengthening before leaving the waiting room

Habakkuk's experience with God once again takes on a poetic and encouraging tone: "The Sovereign LORD [...] makes me as surefooted as a deer, able to tread upon the heights" (Habakkuk 3:19).

The doe is able to climb hills and jump over obstacles without difficulty. The shape of its hind hooves prevents it from slipping, even on steep terrain or on the stony, muddy surface that surrounds the streams where it often drinks water.[1] Its front hooves give it amazing mobility for quick half-turn movements. It can reach speeds of more than 20 miles per hour and leap almost 10 feet high.

Habakkuk could have given up on trusting the Father. The disappointment and initial lack of acceptance of God's sovereignty in choosing the Babylonians as Judah's executioners could have dampened the prophet's spiritual relationship. Instead, he draws on the deer's exceptional abilities to poetically express his security and confidence in God's sovereign presence and power. He could have slipped, but like the deer he managed to jump over the hurdle of fear, panic, and the dreadful feeling caused by God's silence.

But it should also be noted that this steadfastness was achieved during the time he remained in the waiting room. He gained resilience and strength as he turned entirely to God. It is the same with the deer. As a fawn, its feet are neither strong nor agile. Strength and agility come with time and experience in walking up steep and difficult paths.

Even in the face of the Babylonians' immorality and cruelty, and despite his confusion, Habakkuk did not lose sight of the fact that God was on his throne contemplating the situation. Like the prophet, our steadfastness comes from the certainty that the Lord is acting, listening to, and caring for his own, even if we are unable to perceive his actions at the time.

Celina had a hard time trusting God. Because of Joash's silence and estrangement, she went on a downward spiral and felt abandoned by God. Her husband's silence after he left her for a man hurt her deeply. For a time, she would say, "My faith has emptied out."

> Like the prophet, our steadfastness comes from the certainty that the Lord is acting, listening to, and caring for his own, even if we are unable to perceive his actions at the time.

A downward spiral of faith leads to more loneliness and causes wounds that do not heal. This was Celina's case until a godly friend confronted her, forcing her to admit that she had allowed Joash to become a god in her life.

Celina recognized that she had been basing her happiness on her husband rather than on God. Joash never again directly spoke to her again, but little by little Celina has come to trust in the Lord again. Her stay waiting room has been long, but by focusingi on God, she trusts the day of rest will come.

João Carlos had his moments of anger, resulting from resentment against his former investor. Financial need contributed to the urge to wish evil on the man who had betrayed him. The memory of the betrayal created the muddy stones he needed to step on in order to get through the period in the waiting room. Grievances are like stones covered with mud that can cause us to slip. If we choose revenge, we slip and fall. But finally, the day came when João Carlos was freed from the slippery footsteps of vengeful fantasies. Freedom from the grievance and pain caused by the man who had wronged him came as a consequence of redirecting his focus. He began to look to the silent but present God. He realized and accepted that God had always been present in his business, even with the loss he had suffered, and this gave him assurance that the Lord would lift him up again.

In his watchtower waiting for God's answer, João Carlos saw his faith grow and he extended forgiveness to the former investor. João Carlos created a new app. He doesn't yet have a new investor, but he believes that his "majority partner"— the sovereign God—is investing in his life so that he becomes an app developer shaped by grace. It was an older brother in Christ, experienced in prolonged stays in waiting rooms, who contributed to João Carlos's gradual process of change. This friend had been through similar situations, and by sharing his story with João Carlos and telling him how he had turned to God, John Carlos felt strengthened to forgive and rebuild his business.[2]

Having hinds feet means that even on slippery ground, the focus is not on the unstable surface but on the God who keeps us from slipping. The size of a problem or the delay in seeing it resolved can be a muddy terrain, but we can, like Habakkuk, look to God and confidently skip over the muddy stones.

Acquiring feet like a deer's takes time. And God's time is rarely ours. Only he knows the time needed to strengthen us. When he completes his work in us in the waiting room, the door opens and we step into a deeper relationship with him.

Habakkuk comes to the end of his book joyful, full of faith, and resting in God. His intimacy, presence, and communion with God is very evident when he says: "He makes me as surefooted as a deer, able to tread upon the heights" (Habakkuk 3:19). A deer finds refuge and nourishment in the heights after the exhaustion of climbing the steep mountains. Time in waiting rooms also wears us down and generates feelings of helplessness and neediness. In contrast, when we submit to God's processes, we discover that in the Father there is strength, steadfastness, rest, fulfillment, and belonging.

Rejoicing in the Lord is more than a feeling, it is living each day "upon the heights," knowing that in the Lord's time the waiting room door will open up to a room where a banquet of encouragement, rest, and provision for a new phase of life will be served. It means to have the discipline to pray, to remember the deeds of the Lord, to accept divine sovereignty as a loving act, and to believe that God loves us and keeps his promises. This exercise produces the joy which Habakkuk refers to in verse 18 and which he went on to enjoy as one of the virtues of the fruit of the Spirit, presented in Galatians 5:22-23. No one is capable of generating them on their own. The Spirit, on his own initiative, fills us with love, joy, peace, patience, kindness, goodness, faithfulness, gentleness, and self-control.

We will never be free from troubles even in high places, but we can rest in God and be content. William Barcley wrote in his book *The Secret of Contentment*: "You will not be truly content until you learn to be content in every situation that you face in life." [3] Thus, when God takes us out of the waiting room, surely the greatest joy is not to have the problem solved, but to have discovered the God we never really knew!

When our son finally left the hospital, the prognoses were not the best. He might not be able to hear, speak, or develop fine motor skills. Perhaps he wouldn't be able to attend school at all. We only had one choice: look to God. As it turned out, our son was a late learner and experienced difficulties with motor coordination. But in his teens, he became a skilled basketball player and won awards and honors for his athletic skills. At first, we thought he'd never finish high school, but today he's a master's candidate after studying abroad. There are still some aftereffects, but Teca and I are hopeful that one day God will complete the miracle. And if he does not complete it, he will not cease to be our God. He will continue to be the God of our salvation (Habakkuk 3:18). Because of this, we named our son Raphael, which means "God heals."

> Thus, when God takes us out of the waiting room, surely the greatest joy is not to have the problem solved, but to have discovered the God we never really knew!

There's no denying that we often cried out and questioned God. As a pastor, I have learned that my family and I are not immune to difficult or desperate situations, but the time spent in waiting rooms has taught both me and my wife that God is completely trustworthy. We have learned that we are vulnerable to the pain of waiting rooms, and we should not hide our suffering, for it allows other people to become instruments of God's comfort. Spending time with other people in waiting rooms has been a learning experience for me and my wife, for we believe we need to be there for those who are currently going through what we have experienced, whether it is to encourage or to receive encouragement.

> You are not alone in your waiting room. You are actually in a room full of hope.

Are you in the waiting room? Then believe that God will do the same in your life, taking you from despair to hope, taking you to high places in your relationship with him. You are not alone in your waiting room. You are actually in a *room full of hope*. The clock may have stopped, the air conditioning may be broken, and the silence may be deafening, but God is there with you. With a serene and paternal voice, full of love, he whispers to us: "I will never abandon you. You can trust me."

Notes

Introduction

[1] Little is known of the history of the prophet Habakkuk. Considering his message is given in the context of the Babylonian invasion, he assuredly witnessed King Josiah's spiritual reforms and the moral, political, and spiritual collapse of the nation of Judah under the reign of Jehoiakim. This occurred around the years 609 to 598 BC. Habakkuk was a contemporary of the prophets Jeremiah, Nahum, and Zephaniah, who also witnessed Judah's decline.

Chapter 1

[1] The word used by Habakkuk conveys the idea of distance or perpetuity—something that remains infinitely unchanged. See entry 1565 in R. L. Harris, G. L. Archer Jr., and B. K. Waltke (eds.), *Theological Wordbook of the Old Testament*, p. 645.

[2] The meaning of the verb "to cry out" in the Bible always carries the idea of a cry for help in times of despair and desolation. See entry 570 in R. L. Harris, G. L. Archer Jr., & B. K. Waltke (eds.), *Theological Wordbook of the Old Testament*, p. 248.

[3] Habakkuk uses the Hebrew word *pûg*, which has the sense of paralysis, fatigue, weariness, inability to function normally, or even physical weakness.

[4] God describes the Babylonians as those who "conquer other lands." This expression can also be translated as those who "rob" or "take houses that are not theirs." This perspective increased pressure on the prophet. Houses and land were the most valuable material elements for the people, for they represented the fruit of God's covenant with Abraham, Isaac, and Jacob. See K. L. Baker. *Micah, Nahum, Habakkuk, Zephaniah*, vol. 20, p. 299-300.

[5] See the Greek word *parresia* in *Theological Dictionary of the New Testament (Little Kittel)*, p. 871-876. There is a strong connotation of complete transparency before a judge, an unwavering confidence, a courage to be and to speak. See also H. Schlier, G. Kittel, G. W. Bromiley, and G. Friedrich (eds.), *Theological Dictionary of the New Testament*, p. 884.

[6] The word "rock," used by Habakkuk, has the connotation of safety and refuge when referring to God, as in Psalm 89:26 and in Deuteronomy 32:15. J. E. Hartley. Entry 1901. R. L. Harris, G. L. Archer Jr., and B. K. Waltke (eds.), *Theological Wordbook of the Old Testament*, p. 762.

[7] John Piper, "Don't Waste Your Cancer."

Chapter 2

[1] Larry Crabb, *When God's Ways Make No Sense*, p. 33.

[2] P. 15.

[3] P. 59.

[4] Jerry Bridges, *Trusting God*. NavPress, 2016, p. 90.

[5] Mark uses the Greek word *sozo,* which has a double meaning of physical healing and spiritual salvation. This is confirmed by the context, as the evangelist records that Bartimaeus then followed Jesus (10:52).

[6] In this text, God promises to establish the throne of David forever. It is understood from this statement that the Messiah would come from the descendants of David, which in fact happened.

Chapter 3

[1] The verb *sāpâ* carries the idea of being completely alert to a situation or of not being taken by surprise. See *Theological Wordbook of the Old Testament*, entry 1950. See also *Dictionary of Biblical Languages*, Hebrew, entry 7595, Logos Bible Software.

[2] *My Weakness for His Strength, Vol. 1.*

[3] *Bíblia Sagrada Na Jornada com Cristo*, p. 1112.

[4] Johannes P. Louw, Eugene A. Nida. *Greek-English Lexicon of the New Testament: Based on Semantic Domains.*

[5] The verb used by Habakkuk in the Hebrew strongly gives the idea of "standing firm," "going against," "not giving up," or "taking a stand." W. Gesenius, and S. P. Tregelles, *Gesenius' Hebrew and Chaldee Lexicon to the Old Testament Scriptures*, p. 360.
[6] *Confiança inabalável*, São Paulo: Mundo Cristão, 2016.

Chapter 4
[1] *Counterfeit Gods*, p. 15.
[2] See Exodus 16:7,10; 24:17, where the presence of God also carries the idea of power and judgment.

Chapter 5
[1] *When God's Ways Make No Sense*, p. 248.
[2] *Confiança inabalável*, p. 13.
[3] The verb used by Habakkuk contains the idea of resting, sitting, placing oneself at ease, and even sighing after a time of rest. *Theological Wordbook of the Old Testament*. Entry 1323, Logos Bible Software.
[4] See Exodus 5:3; 9:15; Leviticus 26:25; Numbers 14:12; Deuteronomy 28:21; 32:24; 2 Samuel 24:15; Jeremiah 14:12.

Conclusion
[1] *Deer Anatomy — Legs/Feet*. Available on: <www.huntingnet.com>. Accessed: 13 December 2018.
[2] 2 Corinthians 1:3-4.
[3] *The Secret of Contentment*, p. 29.

Bibliography

Armerding, C. E. (1986). "Habakkuk." In F. E. Gaebelein (ed.), *The Expositor's Bible Commentary: Daniel and the Minor Prophets*. Vol. 7. Grand Rapids: Zondervan.

Assis, Helder. *Aprendendo com a corça*. Available on <https://estudos.gospelmais.com.br/aprendendo-com-a-corca.html>. Accessed: 14 December 2018. (Translated title: *Learning from the Deer*).

Barclay, William B. *The Secret of Contentment*. Phillipsburg, NJ: P&R Publishing.

Bíblia Sagrada Na Jornada com Cristo. São Paulo: Mundo Cristão, 2018.

Bíblia Sagrada Tradução King James Atualizada, Edição de Estudo 400 anos. São Paulo: Abba Press and Sociedade Bíblica Ibero-Americana, 2002.

Brannan, R. and Loken, I. *The Lexham Textual Notes on the Bible (Ruth 4:5)*. Bellingham, WA: Lexham Press, Logos Bible Software, 2014.

Bridges, Jerry. *Trusting God*. NavPress, 2016.

Bridges. *Is God Really In Control?: Trusting God in a World of Hurt*. Tyndale House, 2014.

Bromiley, G. W.; Friedrich, G. and Kittel, G. (eds.). *Theological Dictionary of the New Testament*. Grand Rapids: Eerdmans, Logos Bible Software, 1964.

Cassel, P.; Lange, J. P.; Schaff, P. and Steenstra, P. H. *A Commentary on the Holy Scriptures: Ruth*. Bellingham: Zondervan, electronic version, Logos Bible Software, 2008.

Crabb, Larry. *When God's Ways Make No Sense*. Grand Rapids: Baker, 2018.

Fitzpatrick, Elyse. *Idols of the Heart: Learning to Long for God Alone.* Phillipsburg, NJ: P & R Publishing, 2016.

Gesenius, W. and Tregelles, S. P. *Gesenius' Hebrew and Chaldee Lexicon to the Old Testament Scriptures.* Faithlife. Logos Bible Software, 2003.

Keller, Timothy. *Counterfeit Gods: The Empty Promises of Money, Sex, and Power, and the Only Hope that Matters.* New York: Penguin, 2009.

Kennedy, James. *Truths that Transform.* Grand Rapids: Baker, 1996.

Kent, H. A. *Philippians.* In Gaebelein, F. E. (ed.). *The Expositor's Bible Commentary.* Grand Rapids: Zondervan, 1986.

Lenski, R. C. H. *The Interpretation of St. Paul's First and Second Epistle to the Corinthians.* Minneapolis: Augsburg, 1963.

Louw, J. P. and Nida, E. A. *Greek-English Lexicon of the New Testament: Based on Semantic Domains.* New York: United Bible Societies, Logos Bible Software, 1996.

O'Brien, P. T. *The Epistle to the Philippians: A Commentary on the Greek Text.* Grand Rapids: Eerdmans, Logos Bible Software, 1991.

Piper, John. *Não desperdice seu câncer (Don't Waste Your Cancer).* Available on <http://www.monergismo.com/textos/sofrimento/desperdice_cancer_piper.htm>. Accessed: 14 December 2018.

Reed, J. W. *Ruth.* In: Walvoord, J. F. and Zuck, R. B. (eds.). *The Bible Knowledge Commentary: An Exposition of the Scriptures.* Vol. 1. Wheaton: Victor Books, 1985.

Sayão, Luiz. *O problema do mal no Antigo Testamento: O caso de Habacuque (The Problem of Evil in the Old Testament: The Case of Habakkuk).* São Paulo: Hagnos, 2005.

Swanson, J. *Dictionary of Biblical Languages with Semantic Domains: Hebrew (Old Testament).* Bellingham: Logos Research Systems, electronic edition, Logos Bible Software, 1997.

Wells, Mike. *My Weakness for His Strength* (Vol. 1). Littleton, CO: Abiding Life Press, 2011.

Zágari, Maurício. *Confiança inabalável (Unshakeable Trust).* São Paulo: Mundo Cristão, 2016.

About the author

Lisânias Moura is senior pastor at the Morumbi Baptist Church, in São Paulo, where he has served on the pastoral team since 1993. He is responsible for developing the church's vision, preaching, and leading the presbytery, in addition to his pastoral ministry. He holds a BA in pastoral ministry and a master's in theology from Dallas Theological Seminary. Before beginning his pastoral ministry at the Morumbi Baptist Church, he was a professor during ten years at the Word of Life Biblical Seminary in Atibaia, São Paulo. In addition to *A sala da espera de Deus*, (*God's Waiting Room*), he is the author of *Cristão Homoafetivo?* (*A Homoaffective Christian?*) and *Famílias imperfeitas, graça perfeita* (*Imperfect Families, Perfect Grace*), all published by Mundo Cristão. He is married to Teca, and has two sons, Daniel and Rafael, as well as a daughter-in-law, Liana, Rafael's wife.